THE CHR

OF

55 SQUADRON

R.F.C. AND R.A.F.

BY L. MILLER

The Naval & Military Press Ltd

in association with

The Imperial War Museum
Department of Printed Books

NOTICE

The Air Council is in no way responsible for this book or its contents.

L. M.

Published jointly by
The Naval & Military Press Ltd
Unit 10 Ridgewood Industrial Park,
Uckfield, East Sussex,
TN22 5QE England
Tel: +44 (0) 1825 749494
Fax: +44 (0) 1825 765701
www.naval-military-press.com

and

The Imperial War Museum, London
Department of Printed Books
www.iwm.org.uk

In reprinting in facsimile from the original, any imperfections are inevitably reproduced and the quality may fall short of modern type and cartographic standards.

Printed and bound by Antony Rowe Ltd, Eastbourne

E PLURIBUS UNUM.

THE CHRONICLES OF 55 SQUADRON

R.F.C. AND R.A.F.

BY

L. M.

"When you are old and gray and full of sleep,
And nodding by the fire, take down this book,
And slowly read . . ."

W. B. YEATS.

Printed and bound by Antony Rowe Ltd, Eastbourne

DEDICATED TO THE MEMORY

OF

THOSE WHO HAVE MADE THEIR LAST LONG FLIGHT.

L. M.

"They went with songs to the battle, they were young,
Straight of limb, true of eye, steady and aglow.
They were staunch to the end against odds uncounted,
They fell with their faces to the foe.

They shall not grow old, as we that are left grow old,
Age shall not weary them, nor the years condemn.
At the going down of the sun and in the morning
We will remember them.

They mingle not with their laughing comrades again;
They sit no more at familiar tables of home;
They have no lot in our labour of the day-time:
They sleep beyond England's foam."

LAURENCE BINYON.

FOREWORD

"IN my stars I am above thee; but be not afraid of greatness: some are born great, some achieve greatness, and some have greatness thrust upon them."

In suchlike words did I find myself detailed by higher authority to compile the Squadron's history—indeed was "greatness thrust upon me"!

However, in Cologne on January 17, 1919, *on no other* day than the ex-Kaiser's birthday, I first put pen to paper, pleased with the incongruous situation.

The history, such as it is, was completed, with the exception of notes, and went into official circulation on March 5th, 55 Squadron's Birthday.

In the main story names are omitted in order to be impartial and to avoid inadvertently advertising the few at the expense of the Squadron as a whole.

The revival of old memories in the course of writing these chronicles has given me much pleasure, and with the hope that the same pleasure will be yours, I now ask you to read on.

Cheerio!

LEONARD MILLER.

ST. ANDRÉ-AUX-BOIS,
St. Patrick's Day, 1919.

CONTENTS

ROYAL FLYING CORPS:

ROYAL AIR FORCE:

ILLUSTRATIONS

The Chronicles of 55 Squadron

ROYAL FLYING CORPS

England.

The war history of any squadron really only commences overseas, and therefore very little will be said of probationary days in England.

The Squadron was first formed at Castle Bromwich in 1916 as a Training Squadron, with Avros, B.E.2C's, etc., and subsequently moved to Lilbourne, near Rugby.

During the early part of 1917 the machines with which the Squadron was to go on Active Service began to arrive. This machine was the De Havilland 4, fitted with Rolls-Royce engine. The machine was a two-seater, and though originally designed as a fighter, became in course of time a general purposes bus.

There appears to have been some rivalry between 55 and 49 Squadrons (the latter were at Dover) for precedence to proceed to France, both squadrons owning D.H.4's and a certain amount of the very necessary technical stores; but Fortune smiled on the former, and at the end of February, 1917, 55 found itself in that wonderfully chaotic state through which every squadron passes before proceeding overseas. There is the collecting of personnel from all parts of the British Isles, "obtaining" mobilization stores, and generally getting into a confused state of excitement to which the only solution is, "to proceed forthwith" to France and get straightened out, out there. The Adjutant during these days develops a terse diction and a liverish temperament, only to recover overseas as a "Recording Officer." The Equipment Officer and his Staff are unapproachable and develop a pronounced clutching hand and then disappear with the transport, to arrive by devious ways in France with as much as possible of, if not more than, what they started with. The exalted beings, the pilots, are enjoying Embarkation Leave prior to deigning to fly their machines to France, while the new and unqualified observers stand about in the hangars, speculating as to the merits of the machines and the ability of their pilots-to-be to fly them.

The whereabouts of the Commanding Officer is unknown, but can be surmised, —officially, he has gone to see some one at Adastral House.

All these things happen, but to what degree in the case of 55 it would be unwise to say.

However, it survived.

March, 1917.

On Sunday, March 4th, the personnel, consisting of such as could not fly, or be flown, to France, proceeded from Lilbourne station to Rugby. The Medical Officer and his dog saw them off. At Rugby innumerable ladies were waiting for one last glimpse of them, but these were eventually left far behind as the train sped to Euston.

The personnel proceeded to Victoria and then parted to various rest billets, to meet again the following morning and proceed to Folkestone by the train about 7.30 a.m., which most people know only too well.

France.

The crossing of the Channel was uneventful.

At Boulogne no flags were flying to greet them; in fact, the Railway Transport Officer was not expecting them and did not know where they ought to be sent—and did not seem to care, which was discouraging.

The following day, however, the personnel forgathered in the evening and left for Etaples, where they detrained at about midnight and spent an exceedingly cold night in tents.

The next day was spent in getting to Candas, which was the desired destination, and not far from Doullens.

Fienvillers.

The aerodrome was at Fienvillers. From here one could see the gun-flashes on the distant sky and hear the rumble of far-off guns.

Thanks to the hospitality of the resident squadrons, Nos. 19, 27, and 57, all were made comfortable, and for the first fortnight the officers were distributed among their three Messes, and were made very much at home there.

No. 2 Aircraft Depot was alongside the aerodrome, and thither each day pilgrimages were made to see the latest British machines and a Hun aeroplane, an Albatross Scout, which had been shot down and was there under guard, though it could be viewed after compliance with certain formalities. Souvenir hunting was not allowed.

During this time bad weather was holding up the machines in England, but on the 10th of March they began to arrive, and, at the same time, the Squadron moved into its own quarters, a number of Nissen huts in an orchard, behind 27 Squadron's hangars.

On the arrival of all the machines things settled down quickly: pilots selected their observers, Flight Commanders appointed their officers in charge of guns, bombs, cameras, etc., and a general air of there being a war on was worn by all.

In those early days the "buses" had names painted on them. In B Flight one found such names as Niobe, Diana, Dido, Hermione, Penelope, and Atalanta, while a Bacchus, a Pegasus, and a Mars were the most interesting names to be found in A and C Flights. Another fancy feature was the painting of the wheel-covers distinctive colours, of which A had white, B blue, and C red. Later on some one tried red, white, and blue all at once, but his attempt at patriotism was crushed by a caustic telephone call from the Wing.

As yet there were no war worries beyond the disturbing of one's slumbers by 57

Squadron's early morning patrol, as their F.E.2D's rumbled like heavy goods trains over the arched roof of one's Nissen hut, or by Hun prisoners mending the road outside the orchard, to the annoyance of one sleepy and irate pilot, from whom ' those early worms got the bird."

An outbreak of measles occurred, and left one unhappy hut isolated for ten days.

Summer time commenced on the 24th of March, and mulcted one of an hour's rest.

Meanwhile impatience was beginning to be shown by all, for each day one saw the Spads of 19 Squadron, the F.E.2D's of 57, and the Martinsydes of 27 leave on their respective duties, and one looked to the day when the pale-blue flag indicating 55 Squadron would be run up, giving it precedence on the aerodrome with a formation bound for the lines.

April, 1917.

At last, after a tentative " peep at the war " with a " line patrol " on the 3rd of April, the Squadron was considered ready to make its debut.

On Maunday Thursday, the 5th of April, the first shows started out. One was to have been a reconnaissance to Lille, but clouds caused the formation to be broken up, and the attempt had to be abandoned. The other, a bomb raid on St. Amand, likewise encountered bad weather, and though the bombs, forty-eight twenty-pounders, were dropped on the "right side" of the lines, they were not on St. Amand.

The next day a raid was carried out with success on Valenciennes.

The 8th was Easter Day, when Valenciennes was again the target. In addition to this, four machines set out to bomb the Château Hardenpont, near Mons, of which one returned after crossing the lines, leaving three to carry on. These three successfully attained their objective, but were attacked on the way home, with the result that one machine alone recrossed "the lines" and there crashed, the pilot and observer, unfortunately, dying of wounds and injuries received.

The Battle of Arras began next day; indifferent weather, however, followed, and the next raid was not until the 23rd, the objective being Boue.

The next day La Briquette aerodrome was bombed; this lay on the outskirts of Valenciennes. Enemy aircraft attacked, however, and caused two casualties.

The 28th of April proved a good show, according to accounts received later, and indicated no small skill on the part of the leader, for, from the lines to the objective, the path lay over clouds and the earth was visible only in small patches. The cloud banks were cleared on the return near Péronne. The exact spot could hardly have been recognized by an observer, but, the leader's machine being fitted with a camera, a plate was exposed immediately the earth appeared again, and the Intelligence Department was subsequently able to identify the place on the map. This was the first bomb raid on which a camera was taken, cameras having previously been confined to reconnaissance work.

The next day Valenciennes was again the objective.

In the Press, in a résumé of the work done during the month of April, the following paragraph appeared :—

On April 7th, Easter Saturday, the R.F.C. in France fought one of their greatest actions in the war during the opening of the Battle of Arras. It was officially admitted that twenty-eight British machines were missing on that day. The Germans claimed forty-four victims in all, including French machines, and their official communiqués stated that some entire squadrons were destroyed. Our own official communiqués showed later that, between April 3rd and April 9th inclusive, forty-nine of our machines were missing in the week. It became known later that among these were several of at least two brand-new types of British machines which were only put into service for the first time during that week.

One of the " brand-new types of British machines," of course, was the D.H.4, for 55 had the distinction of being the first squadron to use it in France, and on its performance with the Squadron rested the decision as to whether the output of this type should be increased or abandoned.

In view of results it can be safely said that the D.H.4 was a success, for the R.F.C. fitted out several other squadrons with it later on, and all did well, as also did the R.N.A.S. with theirs.

Incidentally a subsequent paragraph is worth while quoting to record a fact not generally known :—

On April 16th the *London Gazette* announced that His Majesty the King had been pleased to become Colonel-in-Chief of the R.F.C.

May, 1917.

Spring had now properly arrived, and advantage was taken of the lengthening days by members of the Squadron for indulging in pedestrianism.

To the neighbouring small town of Bernaville many a pilgrimage on foot was made, the objective being a certain shop that stocked gramophone records.

In the village of Fienvillers there were no attractions. Among a few it was in vogue to visit a small café, commonly known as the "Strand Palace," and there slowly absorb an *apéritif* in the evening before Mess.

On May Day a photographic reconnaissance was made in the area of Busigny.

Valenciennes was raided next day, and followed by raids on Busigny and Brebières.

It now became a custom to make a photographic reconnaissance of an area, and then, should the plates disclose anything of military importance, to follow it up with a bomb raid. In Sir Douglas Haig's dispatch one reads :—

> At the same time bombing machines caused great damage and loss to the enemy by a constant succession of successful raids directed against his dumps, railways, aerodromes, and billets.

The 4th of May was interesting, for on this day the first congratulatory message was received from the General Officer Commanding the Royal Flying Corps, the work consisting of a raid on an aerodrome at La Brayelle and a reconnaissance to Valenciennes.

Three days later Abscon was bombed, and two days later La Briquette. At the same time the Squadron made a small bag in the way of Huns shot and driven down.

The 10th proved a bad day, for on a reconnaissance in the Caudry-Neuvilly area enemy aircraft were encountered, and one of the D.H.4's went down in flames. On the same day photography was done around Cantin, and in the evening a message of cheer came from the G.O.C.

During the relief from work which the indifferent weather occasionally afforded the Squadron, many and varied were the amusements. "Joy-rides" to Amiens, Abbeville, Doullens, and the vicinity of the trenches were frequent. The last-named trips resulted in German hand-grenades and other dangerous souvenirs being collected in large quantities. These, of course, had to be let off at the most inopportune moments, midnight preferably, giving the signal for a battle with Véry lights and a raid on some poor unfortunate and peaceable hut and the shooting up of their water-cans (disused petrol tins) with revolvers. If the mood varied, a visit would be made by the one Mess to the other, for the Squadron was divided in the early days into two Messes. Here so-called music held sway. Jazz bands are a more modern production, but it is absurd to suggest that they are an improvement in either volume or cacophony on the noises produced in A and C Mess at Fienvillers.

One rose in the morning to the strains of a gramophone rendering " Louana Lou," which was so popular with a certain pilot that he would stroll over in the morning, pyjama-clad, to the anteroom to start it up, so that he could shave to it. " Hullo, my Dearie," ran a close second to it, and it can hardly be possible that those who heard either of these there will not, on hearing them now, recall an orchard with its fruit trees, pink and white, with spring blossom, in which were scattered many Nissen huts, each containing half a dozen very good fellows, the memory of many of whom one recalls with a sigh, for they have done their last long flight.

On the 20th the ball started rolling again, and Cantin was bombed.

On the 23rd an attempt was made on

Busigny, but had to be abandoned, though the following day it proved successful. This was followed by another visit to Cantin, and an especially good reconnaissance to Mons.

Two days later a raid on Bohain, the next day on Brebières and a reconnaissance to Solesmes, and May was almost over.

The 31st was moving day. Of course it had to be, for after laborious toil a cinder tennis-court had been made, and the ante-room of No. 1 Mess, which was a Nissen hut, had been raised three feet and painted in wonderful colours. In fact, everything was going very well, and—one moved!

Just prior to moving, 55 presented its next-door neighbours, 57 Squadron, with one of its D.H.4's, while 27 gave them a Martinsyde, for the F.E.2D was now going out of fashion. 57 began to practise strenuously with their new machine, for, having flown pushers hitherto, they needed experience with tractors. That the forward visibility of a tractor as compared with a pusher is by no means as good was well illustrated by one pilot who, hastening to land with thoughts of lunch, failed to notice a haystack, which he decapitated with great success, but with disastrous results to his "tinsyde," though, luckily, no ill-effects to himself.

The Battle of Arras had ceased in its intensive character on May 5th, and preparations were already afoot for an attack by infantry on the Messines-Wytschaete ridge. It was in this connection, though not realized at the time, that the change of aerodromes was ordered.

The move passed off very well. The transport left early in the morning, and the machines about two in the afternoon, after waiting for the weather.

It is submitted that this was the first time in the history of aviation that groceries were delivered by air; for each machine had its share of Mess provender in the shape of half a dozen tins of apricots, salmon, and even bully beef, in order to avoid, in the event of arrival before the transport, the awful necessity of waiting for a meal.

The flight was made in three-quarters of an hour to an aerodrome, not far from St. Omer, called Boisdinghem, and would have been quite satisfactory and uneventful had not a bad accident occurred to one of the last machines to land, with fatal results.

June, 1917.
Boisdinghem.

The first two days after the move were spent in flying in formation over the country behind the lines.

Such flights generally comprised a circuit on the following lines:—St. Omer, Cassel, Poperinghe, Bergues, Dunkirk, Calais, and home again.

Flying over the Channel was very interesting, with the shipping like toy boats below one.

From a height of 18,000 feet it was possible to see four countries at once—France on one's right, England's white cliffs on one's left, and ahead lay the Belgian coast with Zeebrugge Mole jutting out from it, and beyond, in the distance, Holland; Flushing and the mouth of the Scheldt being distinguishable.

On June 3rd a preliminary photographic reconnaissance was made to Courtrai and district. Then followed a busy spell, for, as Sir Douglas Haig remarks in his dispatch:—

As the date for the attack (Messines) drew near, fine weather favoured the work of our airmen.

Raids on Inglemunster and Iseghem and reconnaissances to Bruges and Ghent, Lille and Roubaix, were the day's work for the 4th; raids on Marcke and Bisseghem and a reconnaissance to Ath and Audenarde for the 5th; three successive raids on the 6th to Reckem aerodrome; three on Ramignies Chin and three on Coucou aerodrome kept every one occupied on the 7th.

The G.O.C., 2nd Army, sent his congratulations that night.

Next morning at daybreak the Boche hutments in Holboch Wood received special attention; a reconnaissance along the Belgian coast set out, but had to be abandoned, as also the following day, though a second reconnaissance to Melle, near Ghent, and Ath was successful.

It should perhaps have been mentioned before that the Squadron belonged to the 9th Wing, which was directly under the orders of Headquarters, Royal Flying Corps, without the intermediary of a Brigade Headquarters.

Unlike an Army or Corps Squadron, it was fortunate enough to have allotted to it quite a number of shows in the form of either photographic reconnaissances or bomb raids of a unique and important nature.

In the 9th Wing also were the crack Scout Squadrons.

On the 10th the Belgian coast reconnaissance was again attempted, but proved unsuccessful.

Though at first reconnaissances were done by a formation, one machine with the camera and the others acting as escort, it had now become the practice to send out solo machines, which relied on height for their protection; the answer to that futile riddle, "Why does a mouse when it spins?" "Because the higher the fewer" (Huns), at last seemed to find a useful application.

The 11th of June was eventful, for on it the first award came through in the shape of a Military Cross for the Commander of A Flight.

The next day reconnaissances to Deynze and the Belgian coast set out, the latter again unsuccessful.

Contrary to superstition, the 13th proved a lucky day, for at last the Belgian coast reconnaissance was completed, eighteen plates being exposed at 18,500 feet.

This reconnaissance was particularly required in view of the relief by British troops of the French holding the coast sector from St. George's to the sea, which resulted later in the Lombaertzyde attack. In addition, the coastal aerodromes, from which the Hun raids on London started, and the submarine bases at Nieuport, Ostend, and Bruges came thereby under the eye of the Intelligence Department.

The next four days were confined to reconnaissances of different areas, followed by a raid on the 17th on Provin.

" Dud " weather followed until the end of the month, with one attempt at a reconnaissance on the 27th, which was partially successful, the objective being the location of the big gun which had been bombarding Dunkirk, known as the Leugenboom Gun. The machine that did this reconnaissance made a spectacular return in a thunderstorm, and soon after a message of congratulation came from the G.O.C., ending with the words, " I was getting anxious." The personal interest of Headquarters was naturally much appreciated by all concerned.

July, 1917.

July began with a raid on Dorignies on the 2nd and a reconnaissance to Ostend. In this instance, on its return, the machine forced-landed on the coast near Dunkirk, but the observer, thanks to the services of a squadron near which the landing had been made, turned up in a R.E.8, hugging his precious plates.

The next day Dorignies was again the objective, and the reconnaissance, done at 20,000 feet, included Leugenboom, Bruges, and Ghistelles, the last-named being an important Hun aerodrome. The photographs of Leugenboom showed the damage done by the night-bombing of 100 Squadron, who flew F.E.2B's.

After an interval of two days, on the 6th Dorignies again received a visit, and a reconnaissance was made of the Herseaux-Pecq area.

The next day comprised an area reconnaissance, a bomb raid to Ramignies Chin, and a special patrol for His Majesty King George, who was in France and was visiting, among other places, St. Omer, where No. 1 Aircraft Depot was situated.

Now that high-altitude solo reconnaissances were of frequent occurrence, oxygen-breathing apparatus was fitted to machines, and, though opinions differed at the time as to the real usefulness of this additional "gadget," it proved that ultimately the pilot and observer who dispensed with it felt the effects of altitude flying very much more than they who had consistently used it, and also that the former were liable to a sudden breakdown, possibly in the air.

Four days after the Royal Patrol, a long-distance bomb raid set out for Mons and another for the railways around Arseele, both of which were successful. However, a reconnaissance to Gontrode, though attempted twice, was only partially successful, and another on the Belgian coast had to be left incomplete owing to clouds, which showed how the weather varied in different parts.

It will be noticed that the objectives are at times widely apart, and this added greatly to the interest of the work and did away with the monotony of flying over the same sector of the country day after day.

The following day raids to La Briquette aerodrome, near Valenciennes, and the railways and sidings at Eyne, with a reconnaissance of the Moorseele area, filled the bill.

On the 13th operations consisted of raids to Orchies and Eyne, while the reconnaissance to Gontrode of the 11th was again attempted and completed, including Melle sidings and the St. Denis Westrem aerodrome, one of the Huns' starting-places for the air-raids on London.

During the week some interesting experiments were made, using machines of 70 Squadron, who were on the same aerodrome and who flew Sopwith two-seaters, in connection with wireless telephony. It was curious to "listen in" on the ground to two machines out of sight in the clouds exchanging back-chat.

The weather that followed proved useless for photographic work, though on the 14th a bomb raid was carried out on La Briquette, followed on the 16th and 17th by others on Ledeghem and Somain respectively.

On the 20th Somain was visited again, also Ramignies Chin, and the following day La Brayelle and the ammunition dump at Arleux.

By the 22nd the weather had improved sufficiently to allow of two long raids, as a consequence of the features disclosed by the photographs of the 13th, to the railway sidings at Melle and the Zeppelin shed at Gontrode. On this raid one of the D.H.4's failed to return, making a short-cut to internment for the duration of the war by forced-landing in Holland.

The same day, which was Sunday, the

Huns raided England early in the morning, and the alarm came through about nine o'clock.

Six D.H.4's left the ground as soon as possible, and flew by way of Dunkirk out over the North Sea, to intercept the raiders. Unfortunately, though the raiders were sighted well away to the east, it was impossible to reach them. "They had their noses well down and were beetling like stink for home," as was unofficially reported in flying lingo.

To complete a busy day, a reconnaissance was made to Tournai. It was remarkable, all along, how often Sunday proved the reverse of a day of rest.

Gontrode again was the target on the 23rd, in addition to Arseele and Eyne.

The dumps at Lichtervede received attention on the next day, while the first armament officer arrived and could be seen from then onwards strenuously wrestling with recalcitrant Lewis guns, or giving one last word of advice to observers about to leave the ground. One could recognize him across the aerodrome by the remarkable raincoat that he invariably wore.

About this time the Squadron developed a mania for collecting magpies, and spent its spare time digging for worms for them. There was one Flight Commander who had a superstition with regard to them, and invariably saluted them lest bad luck should befall him. Undoubtedly there must have been some slackness in this respect later on, for he was unfortunate enough to have a contretemps with some rockets and rather badly injured his foot. Almost simultaneously the magpies disappeared . . . after all, superstitions are rather silly.

It was also about this time that the semi-official bombing officer, who had a penchant for contriving unearthly and terrifying noises at inopportune moments, on the plea of making sure that the contents of the bombs were all they should be, having frightened himself severely by nearly blowing himself up (apart from being blown up, together with his fellow-conspirators, by Wing Headquarters, whose afternoon nap they had disturbed), found it safer to indulge in lesser excitements, and the Tin Hat Club was formed, which being of a secret nature, will be known only to a select few, but it is necessary to record its existence.

On the 27th Renaix and Gontrode were bombed, and photographic reconnaissances covered the areas around Wieltje and Zillebeke-Houthulst. The latter, being for the artillery, was rather important as a part of the preliminaries to the Third Battle of Ypres, and a reference to it is found in the Commander-in-Chief's dispatch.

> So effective was our counter-battery work that the enemy commenced to withdraw his guns to places of greater security. On this account, and also for other reasons, the date of our attack, which had been fixed for the 25th July, was postponed for three days. This postponement enabled a portion of our own guns to be moved further forward, and gave our airmen the opportunity of locating accurately the enemy's new battery positions.

On this last-mentioned show the Squadron Commander himself piloted the machine which by means of photographs located accurately the enemy's new battery positions.

The following day bombs were dropped on Gontrode and Valenciennes, and by way of a side-show the Commander-in-Chief's camouflaged train was photographed from the air with a new type of oblique camera, to see if its camouflage really was good or not.

During the night a Handley-Page landed

on the aerodrome, and proved a matter of great interest all the following morning. To most of the Squadron it was quite a novelty, as also were the notices on it, "Ostend twice nightly," and suchlike.

The month's work finished on the 29th with a couple of raids on Melle sidings and Wynghene aerodrome respectively; the 30th and 31st were "dud" days.

August, 1917.

August began with rain, and remained too bad for flying until the 10th. Ever since the Squadron had been at Boisdinghem it had been under canvas, and life during this inclement spell was not too pleasant.

On the 3rd the first foreign decoration came through in the form of the Ordre de la Couronne, a Belgian award, which was bestowed upon the Commanding Officer. Prior to this, however, there had been a number of Military Crosses given to Flight Commanders for excellent work done in leading formations on bomb raids in the face of strong opposition by the Hun, and to one flying officer whose reconnaissance work had been "particularly daring and successful."

On August 10th flying began again, and there followed a fortnight which, though not more than usually busy, was the worst in casualties that, up to date, had been the Squadron's misfortune.

Heule aerodrome was raided twice, and the Bruges and Ghent areas were photographed.

The 12th passed with raids on Inglemunster and Abeele, the next day with a raid on Deynze and Mouveaux area reconnaissance.

The following day provided but one raid, on Abeelehoek, and the 15th proved a blank day.

On August 16th a new departure was made in sending out a solo bombing machine, which, by dint of playing hide-and-seek in the clouds, was to avoid hostile aircraft. Unfortunately, the machine failed to return, the pilot landing unhurt, but completely lost, in Hunland; a repetition of the solo bomb raid was not made until over a year afterwards.

A start was made to bomb Heule, but had to be abandoned, though the second attempt proved successful, while in addition Seclin and Courtrai received their quota of bombs.

The next day Inglemunster was the target and Thourout the centre for photographic work.

On the 18th the change was rung by a visit to La Briquette, though the reconnaissance was the same as on the previous day, as again on the following day, accompanied by a raid on Farmars. The 20th was a repetition of the 19th.

The next day was the last working day in August, with raids on Raismes and Ramignies Chin. Then followed a fortnight's bad weather; the month had begun with rain, but now the rain was accompanied by strong winds, with the result that in the early hours ghostly forms clad in raincoats and pyjamas could be seen anxiously adjusting pegs and guy-ropes and endeavouring to prevent the total collapse of their tents. The Mess marquee blew over almost nightly. Speaking of tents calls to mind the weird and wonderful camouflaging done on them, of which the Squadron Equipment Officer's was possibly the most remarkable, with a cow (?) and trees worked into the general scheme.

During the "dud" spell the Squadron was fortunate enough to receive visitors in the form of two concert parties known as the "Dickybirds" and the "Crumps," both of which were very much appreciated.

In addition, a Voisin turned up after lunch one day, in a regular gale of wind, and, as from an aluminium bath-tub, there tumbled three extraordinary figures—one clad entirely in black leather, complete with crash helmet, a second who wore red whiskers and a blue tam-o'-shanter, and the third a scared and chilly mortal in the uniform of one of the Allied navies. In voluble French they explained that they were bound from Paris to Dunkirk, and then he of the red whiskers recognized one of the Flight Commanders, having met him at Port Said earlier in the war, and a touching scene ensued.

Apart from outside amusements of this kind, the spirits of the Mess were kept up by certain happy-hearted songsters who would render "Ragging thro' the Rye" or a staccato version of "Funiculi funicula" on, or without, the slightest provocation. Copious drinks were poured into the piano, which stood the treatment remarkably well.

Little has been said of the other squadron that shared the aerodrome during these busy summer months. Reference has been made to 70 Squadron and their Sopwith two-seaters, but they, after refitting with Camels (a Sopwith single-seater), left, and were replaced by 57 Squadron, who had now forgotten all about "pushers," and considered that they knew as much about the D.H.4 as 55 itself, "Which (as in a definition of Euclid's) is absurd."

The bad weather was responsible for keeping a reconnaissance to Brussels standing by, day after day.

The strenuous summer months could now be considered nearly over, and pilots and observers were able to go to bed, thankful that in the early morning their slumbers would not be rent by the hideous yell of a blaring electric Klaxon horn. Such an instrument of high power was fixed on a pole in the midst of the quarters and was controlled by a switch in the Squadron office. As an effective means of rousing sleepy aviators it cannot be beaten, but there is more than one person now to whom the sound must still be hateful, and, judging by the animosity displayed towards this instrument of torture when its usefulness had ceased to be, that hate must be very deep indeed, for few small objects short of a piece of lace could be so full of holes as this horn was after the Squadron had used it for revolver practice on a certain memorable occasion.

September, 1917.

Early in September the weather began to improve, but it was found that the atmosphere had been affected by the continuous winds, and the known best climbing machine, capable of at least 20,000 feet, when taken on a test flight by the C.O., found its ceiling at a trifle over 18,000 feet. The reason for this it is not proposed to discuss, but the incident remains as an interesting fact and as a basis for argument amongst those who know and those who think they know, samples of whom any Royal Air Force Mess will supply.

On the 11th of September a photographic reconnaissance to Blicquy set out and was away close upon three and three-quarter hours, which was considered at that time no mean flight. The cause of its long absence was still the difficulty in getting height; an altitude of 19,000 feet was attained only after two hours' climbing, whereas a little over half that time usually sufficed. The pilot on this show eventually became a star turn as a leader of long-distance raids, as those who read may learn.

SOLO RECONNAISSANCE.

[From a water-colour by LIEUT. B. F. SANDY.]

The following day the Equipment Officer left the Squadron and removed himself with a wonderful amount of impedimenta to the scene of greater triumphs near Rouen.

The next "job of work," as the C.O. would have termed it, was not until the 22nd, and this was a bomb raid on Bavai, which was unique, in that the machines first flew to the old aerodrome at Fienvillers and there loaded up with bombs, refilled with petrol, and then set out for their objective. Ascq received attention on the same day.

On the 24th three raids were made on Abeele, while photographs were taken of "northern and southern aerodrome areas," as the official operation orders, rather uninterestingly, put it.

The following day the programme consisted of raids on Gontrode, Melle, and Marcke, but a reconnaissance was unlucky enough to run into hostile aircraft; however, it returned safely, though badly shot about.

On the 27th, 28th, and 30th efforts were concentrated on Gontrode, while on the 30th Roulers was bombed as well as the Aeltre area photographed.

Towards the end of the month there had

been a visitor from 27 Squadron in the form of a D.H.4 with a Galloway B.H.P. engine, which aroused a certain amount of interest.

During the month the Squadron concert party, who were known as "The Snails" (the Squadron marking on its Mechanical Transport being a snail), gave their second show. Their first had been produced at Fienvillers, and was a revue entitled "Après la Guerre." Whether they have found life since demobilization anything like that they depicted on the stage it would be interesting to know. The second production was remarkable for its wonderful property Tank, which, having foiled a desperate attack, turned at the psychological moment into a canteen and refreshed the hungry troops.

On the 30th of September a Hun photographic machine came directly over the aerodrome about midday. After dark a night-bomber came very near and dropped a parachute flare, but there was no other damage beyond that to the nerves of those who were watching and waiting for it.

On several occasions previously the Hun night-bombing machines had passed overhead *en route* to Boulogne, but without noticing the aerodrome.

This was situated on fairly high ground, and the attacks on Calais, Dunkirk, and nearer still, at St. Omer and on the large dumps at Audruicq, were plainly visible, and little groups of officers and men would congregate on the aerodrome to watch " flaming onions " and other fireworks that resulted. On one occasion some anxiety was caused by the sound of a machine planing down towards the aerodrome, apparently on the point of releasing its bombs, but just as every one was thinking of burrowing into the smooth and unreceptive surface of the aerodrome the pilot opened up his engine, which all recognized easily as being a " rotary," and as it was known that the Hun bombers did not use this type of engine, by clever deduction it was argued that it must be a Britisher. Next day it was confirmed to have been a night-flying Scout, a Camel, looking for Huns.

There had recently been a rather remarkable flight by Count Laureati in an Italian biplane fitted with a Fiat engine, from Turin to Hounslow, and apparently the Technical Branch of the R.F.C. considered the engine worth while testing with a view to fitting it in the D.H.4 in place of its present engine for use in long-distance bombing.

As a consequence the Squadron's Technical Sergeant-Major was sent to one of the Aircraft Depots, and amongst those in the Squadron whom the change of engines would have affected there was much speculation as to the results of these tests. However, no change in the make of engines ever did take place, though a high-powered series of the same make was eventually installed throughout.

October, 1917.

The first day of October resulted in Gontrode being the objective for both bomb raid and reconnaissance.

The following day two raids went to both Marcke and Bisseghem.

The next day Courtrai and Iseghem were favoured, as again on the 7th.

On the 3rd certain rumours began to go the rounds, and those who knew anything began to be mysterious. The Recording Officer and the Equipment Officer wore worried looks. "Something must be in the wind," said the observant, and the curious began to feel distinctly unsettled. Some one went to St. Omer to the Field Cashier and came back with full particulars: "Every one there knows all about it." He was promptly extinguished by a Pyrenic remark from the C.O.

Then on Sunday, the 7th, came certain people from 25 Squadron spying out the land.

Had anybody only learned the lesson that history repeats itself and remembered how, at Fienvillers, directly the Squadron got comfortable it moved, he would have known all there was to know, for the past weeks had been spent in obtaining and erecting a wonderful hospital Nissen hut for a Mess and anteroom, while everybody was by now well installed in a Nissen hut and all traces of canvas had disappeared.

Strenuous days followed, teeming with all kinds of preparations, which resulted in a move on the 11th. Of the night before leaving it is mooted that no one knows full particulars—if he does, let him for ever hold his peace!

The machines all left by noon, and those who were not flying, together with all the paraphernalia that a squadron and its personnel accumulates, moved by road to St. Omer.

Here by five o'clock all was transhipped to a train, and at seven 55 Squadron started south.

The next morning the train reached Candas

station, hard by Fienvillers aerodrome, and here extra trucks with spare machines, stores, planes, etc., were added, totalling some forty in all. The train proceeded slowly but surely to Amiens, and the environs of Paris, Noisy-le-Sec, were passed through that evening.

The following day the new railhead was reached at 10 a.m. This was a little place called Barisey-la-Côte, between Toul and Neufchateau, which places are in the Departments of Meurthe-et-Moselle and Vosges respectively.

The weather was very wet and transport was sadly lacking, but eventually everything was transported to the new aerodrome at Ochey.

In the meantime the majority of the machines had found their way down, despite the unfavourable weather. On the 11th of October, in fact, five machines had flown from Boisdinghem to Ochey, about two hundred miles, in one flight, which was by no means a bad performance, taking weather conditions as well into consideration.

Ochey.

On Ochey aerodrome No. 16 Naval Squadron (afterwards known as No. 216) with Handley-Pages, and No. 100 with F.E.2B's, were more or less installed. The officers of 55 Squadron were thrust upon the hospitality of the latter, and the men billeted in the village of Thuilley-en-Groseilles, close by in the valley. Neither of the other Squadrons had many machines, and consequently there was much rivalry as to who should get the first show away. It should be remarked that both the others were night-bombing squadrons. The preparations involved, among other things, the blotting out of the white triangle which, when at Boisdinghem, had been used to identify the D.H.4's of 55 from those of 57 and 25 and other squadrons similarly equipped. The Squadron artist designed a new identification mark, consisting of a winged figure gracefully dropping an idealized bomb on to some silhouette factories below. For want of a lay figure, the artist used his own reflection (so those who peeped in at the window said): it is a wonder he did not catch his death of cold. Unhappily, higher authority, possibly not appreciative of high art, decreed "No identification marks at all," and the design survived merely as a cartoon and Mess decoration entitled "Reprisals."

However, on October 17th 55 Squadron sent out the first raid of two formations to Burbach factory, near Sarrebruck, on which 1,792 lbs. of bombs were dropped.

In the French newspapers the next day appeared the following paragraph, the first direct reference to operations carried out by the Squadron :—

AVIONS ANGLAIS SUR SARREBRUCK

COMMUNIQUÉ OFFICIEL BRITANNIQUE.

17 *Octobre*, 23 *Heures* 30.

Nous avons exécuté avec beaucoup de succès, cet après-midi, une expédition de bombardement en territoire ennemi et attaqué une usine à l'ouest de Sarrebruck, à environ soixante-cinq kilomètres au délà de la frontière allemande. De nombreuses bombes ont été jetées avec d'excellents resultats. Des incendies ont été constatés dans l'usine. Tous nos appareils sont rentrés indemnes.

The next day or two were "dud," and the second show was not until the 21st, when a factory west of Bous was the recipient of 2,464 lbs. of bombs. This time hostile aircraft were encountered, and one machine failed to return.

On the evening of October 24th the night-fliers got away, but unfortunately two Handley-Pages failed to return.

Then on the 28th it snowed, and the same night a small fire occurred, completely gutting a workshop lorry.

On the 30th Pirmasens had 2,712 lbs. of bombs dropped on it, the objective being a boot-factory (a subtle method of giving the Huns cold feet). The 31st was a blank day.

Meanwhile preparations were being made at another aerodrome near Tantonville for the reception of the Squadron. The first week or so life was rather uncomfortable, as the three squadrons were isolated from British supply units, and the attempted subsistence on French rations, though an experience, was not appreciated by either officers or other ranks. However, an A.S.C. officer soon put in an appearance, and rations began to improve.

November, 1917.

The 1st of November supplied the one and only raid of the month, the objective being Kaiserslautern. There were no casualties.

Tantonville.

On the 7th the move to Tantonville took place, and the Squadron busied itself in getting as comfortable as possible for the winter, which, reports said, would be rather severe. When the Squadron moved from Ochey it left there accompanied by a dog which had taken a fancy to it, and this fancy was mutual. His name was Roger, and he deserves remembrance in the Squadron's records.

Roger was no ordinary dog. A follower of the teachings of Pythagoras could imagine that Roger was once an old and well-to-do uncle, who, clad in an overcoat with an astrakhan collar, used to favour his small nephews' school with his patronage, for Roger had a penchant for the young, though at times their boisterous behaviour bored him.

Roger was a gourmand and a sybarite. The mere mention of chocolates would hold him fascinated by one's presence, and he would remind one that a great friendship existed between him and oneself, but if one failed to share them with him, he could feign an indifference that was wonderful to see. The best sofa in the Mess was his by right of conquest, and he slept at nights on the foot of the C.O.'s bed.

Roger was conservative and possessed of pronounced prejudices, one of which was a great distaste for all races other than the British. The French, the Cochin Chinese, and the Italians who passed the aerodrome were all the victims of his displeasure, and he would hound them from the precincts of the camp with threats of prosecution for trespassing, though he never stooped to violence.

Roger had one tragic *affaire de cœur*—but why revive so sad a memory? A brighter subject is the interest and enthusiasm he displayed in aviation and bombing the Hun. Few raids left the aerodrome that Roger did not personally see away, chasing each machine until it left the ground and shouting final encouragement to pilot and observer.

For the company of senior officers he showed a marked preference, though he would condescend occasionally to fraternize with lesser stars.

For driving in the C.O.'s touring car he had a positive mania, and the supercilious air he assumed as he sat next to the driver was apt to pique the average flying officer, who was lucky if he could get a "joy-ride" in a light tender.

In the evenings, occasionally, Roger would unbend and entertain the company by playing "Rag the Bag" or "Cuddle the

Cushion," both of which are too technical to explain here and need to be seen to be properly understood, like modern dancing.

His unvarying good temper under the most trying conditions was exemplary, and yet, with all his virtues, Roger was a Hun-dog.

Now this is the alleged origin of Roger: Born and bred in Hun-land, he accompanied his Boche master to the trenches in the Vosges sector, where either he showed his good taste by crossing to the French lines or else was captured. His French captors were blind to his charms, and his dislike for them was obvious. So, representing a mark of esteem for "Gallant British aviators" on the part of the French and with appropriate wording, he was handed over to 100 Squadron.

Apparently Roger did not care for night-bombing, and so became attached officially and sentimentally to 55 Squadron, and left Ochey in its company, as already recorded.

That started the feud.

Under guise of paying a peaceful visit, certain officers of 100 Squadron dined one evening with 55; when they left, Roger was missing.

Enquiry was made by telephone, and an admission was wormed from them that Roger was again at Ochey.

Strategy and tactics were called to aid.

A side-car proceeded to Ochey, in which rode Roger's best friend, but his mission was not to see about a dog, but to confer on matters of a different nature.

Six D.H.4's left the ground on a practice formation, and by chance flew low over Ochey aerodrome.

By a strange coincidence Roger's friend stood chatting by one of the hangars and Roger lurked close by.

A D.H.4 landed and "taxied" towards the hangar. How it happened Roger himself could never explain, but all of a sudden he was whisked from the earth; he found himself in his friend's arms, being carried at the double to the approaching aeroplane. Next moment he was in the arms of the observer in the cockpit of the machine, a second later the D.H.4 was speeding over the aerodrome, and, before the onlookers had grasped the situation, Roger was flying in formation back to Tantonville.

Such was the Rape of Roger, and though other incidents occurred, none was as spectacular as this.

December, 1917.

December was an improvement on the previous month, and was productive of three minor reconnaissances and of five raids as follows :—

On the 5th, Zweibrucken and Saarbrucken, followed on the 6th by one to Burbach and on the 11th by one to Pirmasens.

The star show of the month and of any up to date was on Christmas Eve, when the Baden Aniline Dye Factory at Mannheim was attacked, unfortunately at the cost of one machine missing.

The newspapers supplied the following interesting paragraphs :—

BRITISH NARROWLY MISSED KAISER IN MANNHEIM RAID.

GENEVA, *Wednesday.*

During the British air raid on Mannheim on Christmas Eve, the Kaiser and his Staff had an extremely narrow escape. They were returning from the Verdun front on their way to Berlin, and the Imperial special train passed through Mannheim station a bare hour before the structure was partially wrecked by British bombs.

The train was, in fact, the last to leave Mannheim, and none has since arrived at Bâle from that point. The permanent way has been destroyed for some distance beyond the station, thus cutting off communication with the north.

Two bombs fell on the palace of the Palatinate and one on the suspension bridge which crosses the Neckar. Both structures were badly damaged.

A munitions factory in a northern suburb of the town was blown up, but as most of the workers were on holiday there were few fatalities. A number of persons were killed or injured in the town.

The German newspapers have begun their cry against the wickedness of bombing "harmless open towns."—*Daily Express.*

The Secretary of the War Office made the following announcement :—

December 30*th*.—The following further information about the bombing raid on Mannheim carried out on December 24th has now been received :—

Two of our formations, totalling ten machines, crossed the line at a height of 9,000 feet between 10 and 10.15 a.m. The two formations arrived over the objective almost simultaneously, and, in spite of heavy and accurate anti-aircraft fire, dropped their bombs from a height of over 13,000 feet.

Sixteen 112-lb. bombs and two 230-lb. bombs were dropped in all, four bursts being observed in the main station, several in the Lanz works, two in Ludwigshafen, and several in the munitions factory between Mundenheim and Rheingonnheim, bursts being partially confirmed by photographs taken at the time.

Two formations of enemy aeroplanes were encountered, totalling eleven machines, of which, however, only five reached the height of the bombing machines, and these did not attempt to attack at close range.

The anti-aircraft defences around Mannheim appeared strong, and brought down one of our machines, which was last seen descending under control. In addition, one of our observers was wounded, but reached home safely.

Haze and mist added to the difficulties of the operation, some towns in the Rhine valley being completely covered.

During the month the weather had become much colder, and fuel-foraging parties were the fashion. On obtaining the fuel the next thing was to get it cut up small enough to go into one's stove, but this could be attained by working close to a certain Anglo-Canadian and making futile hacks at the logs. Eventually, in the kindness of his heart, he would take the axe from you and cut the wood up deftly himself; after which you thanked him kindly and withdrew.

The neighbouring village of Xirocourt became a centre for recherché dinners, while the élite discovered a place where snails were to be had in large quantities, and a Snail Club came into being. This club had extraordinary rules, among which fines paid in drinks appeared to predominate.

Inter-squadron football began to be a feature, while several matches were played with French troops billeted in the neighbourhood, until the ground became too hard.

PUNCH, OR THE LONDON CHARIVARI.—JANUARY 2, 1918.

[*By courtesy of* Punch.]

AN EASY CONUNDRUM.

FIRST WATCHER ON THE RHINE. "These accursed British, our so peaceful and cultured Mannheim to bomb!"

SECOND DITTO. "What devil taught them this frightfulness?"

Christmas Day passed happily, finishing with a show by the Squadron concert party entitled " Deux Œufs," and they were by no means bad eggs at that. The concert party were particularly well-dressed on this occasion, having made a find of some excellent dresses in the small town of Mirecourt.

On Boxing Day the thermometer fell to 10 degrees Fahrenheit; the next day snow fell.

The Old Year went out without further incident of any note, and the New Year was commenced with speculations as to whether 1918 would prove the last year of the War or not.

January, 1918.

The cold weather that had set in lasted until Twelfth Night, and then the thermometer went up to 40 degrees Fahrenheit, and it rained. The same day the leader of the first formation in the Mannheim raid received a bar to his Military Cross.

Early in the New Year a change of Armament Officers took place, and the well-groomed one of raincoat fame handed over his worries to an equally harassed " old bean " and proceeded to Home Establishment. A word or two might be said to record the fact that the mounting of two Lewis guns for use by the observer had originated with the Squadron in March, 1917, and had proved its worth in many a sharp skirmish with the Boche. Opinion, however, was not unanimously in favour of the double mountings. Some contended that a single gun was handier and less cumbersome, others liked having a second gun as a stand-by, but objected to the extra weight of gun and ammunition, and so the matter never was decided; some used one type, some the other.

Now followed an uneventful week.

On the 14th weather conditions improved, of which advantage was taken to raid Karlsruhe, upon which a ton or so of bombs was dropped, including a phosphorus bomb, which, though probably not the cause of much damage, appeared on the photographs which were taken over the town, with great effect. Successive plates showed the gradual growth of the cloud of dense white smoke which resulted from it, and spectacularly it was considered a great success. Incidentally, it was the first time that the Squadron had used this type of bomb. The weather remained mild but unsuitable for aerial work, though on the Sunday a little "joy-riding" was indulged in, to the delight of the French villagers, who turned out in their Sunday best to see the flying. By way of a *divertissement* a phosphorus bomb was dropped, and those Frenchmen who were not alarmed by it appreciated the additional side-show very much, with the result that the Sunday gatherings became quite a custom.

A word is due about the aerodrome itself, which was L-shaped, the angle of the letter containing a wood, into which the hangars were recessed and very ingeniously camouflaged.

The aerodrome was loaned from the French, and the work on it had all been done by comic little stocky French colonial troops from Cochin China.

The quarters likewise were in another wood on the other side of the road that passed the aerodrome; these too were well hidden among the trees.

It can be said without fear of contradiction, and on the authority of a senior officer, whose duties had taken him to every aerodrome in France occupied by British squadrons, that this one was quite unique.

From the point of view of surface and

accessibility for landing, however, it could well have been improved upon, for it sloped, it was soft, and in most cases landing had to be made over some high-tension electric wires, with which, luckily, no one at any time collided, but nevertheless they were a constant source of anxiety.

By the 25th the weather improved enough for a reconnaissance to Mars la Tour, and for another on the 27th to Luxembourg, while on the same day Trèves was bombed.

During the month the rumour went round that 55 was losing its Squadron Commander; this proved true, and the Flight Commander of "B" succeeded him. However, the loss was not entire, for the former became its Wing Commander. Since leaving the 9th Wing in the north the Squadron had come under the command of Headquarters, 41st Wing retaining, however, until now, the same Colonel as hitherto.

February, 1918.

The next raid was not until the 12th of February, and then on Offenburg, while on the same day a reconnaissance was made of the Remilly area.

Again an interval; then followed three successive days of hard work. On the 18th and 19th raids were made on Trèves and Thionville, and on the 20th on Pirmasens. Reconnaissances were made on the Remilly-Saarburg area.

No more shows were done that month, though the night-fliers were out on the night of the 26th, when the moon was bright, and landed upon the aerodrome.

Rain and snow supervened.

March, 1918.

As the year progressed additions were made to the personnel of the Squadron by the attachment of a Photographic, an Intelligence, and a Meteorological Officer. A visit to the office of each was a splendid way of killing the morning of a "dud" day. Of course the Stores and Equipment Officer could have been included, but he had terse notices up, peremptorily telling one to "keep out," and he seemed to be afraid of losing things.

Apart from the visiting, there was also the joy of watching the meteorological balloons go up, while the observation of them, with weird and wonderful instruments, by certain aged gentlemen, would have pleased Mr. Heath Robinson immensely.

The 5th of March was the first anniversary

of the Squadron's arrival in France, and a dinner was held at Xirocourt by a few of the older members to celebrate it.

The next day the weather was good enough for a show, but the surface of the aerodrome after the rain and thawing snow was so soggy that the machines, after attempting to "taxi" out and sinking into mud up to the axles, had to be taken back to the hangars and the show abandoned.

A visitor in the shape of a three-engined Caproni landed during the afternoon, but luckily managed to get away again.

On the 9th, however, a successful raid was made upon Mainz. The following day Stuttgart was the objective for the raid, with Luxembourg for the reconnaissance. In this connection one of the Flight Commanders who was detailed for the work had the cockpit of his machine catch fire in the air. He managed to land, though he crashed, and thanks to promptness on the part of his observer no serious harm resulted to him.

Luxembourg was down for photography again on the 11th.

The 12th was a red-letter day, with the longest distance raid then done, the objective being Coblenz. The leader was the pilot referred to on the 11th of September, 1917, now a Flight Commander. The General Officer Commanding 8th Brigade (which had lately been formed, and under which 41st Wing and the Squadron came) paid a visit to the Squadron to express his satisfaction.

Unfortunately, the following day proved unlucky, for, on a raid to Freiburg, three machines were lost. Petange and Luxembourg were the areas for reconnaissance. The Petange area again was photographed on the 15th.

The raid on Zweibrucken on the 16th proved a "hot show," though luckily no machines were lost. The same day the Distinguished Service Order was bestowed upon the leader of the Coblenz raid, with the following tribute:—

On five occasions during a period of three months he has led formations on long-distance bombing raids, in which, despite bad weather conditions, he has found and bombed his objectives with the most excellent results. All the operations in which he has taken part have proved highly successful, and his capabilities have stood out most prominently. He is a keen and most efficient pilot, and by his courage and determination has set a splendid example to his Squadron.

On St. Patrick's Day the factories at Kaiserslautern were bombed, and the following day Mannheim received its second visitation.

The following Sunday, after a short interval of bad weather, Mannheim was bombed again, and two machines "went missing," one of which was a Deputy Leader's. Also, a Sergeant Observer, a splendid fellow, was brought back by his pilot, dead in his cockpit.

Then followed weather with a tendency to snow, and a short raid to the railways at Metz was all that could be done on the 27th. However, next day Luxembourg was bombed, and proved an easy business, for no Huns were encountered, and even the anti-aircraft defence seemed to have been caught napping.

Easter Day ended March and also the history of 55 Squadron as a unit of the Royal Flying Corps.

During March a total of 24,888 lbs. of bombs was dropped.

ROYAL AIR FORCE

April, 1918.

The next morning, All-fools' Day, every one woke up to find themselves members of the Royal Air Force, as arranged by the Air Ministry.

The first raids as an R.A.F. unit were upon Luxembourg on the 5th. Then a week of no event, and the weather allowed of a show to Metz that, together with four area reconnaissances, which were now known by numbers and so lost their individuality, completed the operations for the month of April.

During the month the first D.H.4 machine with an VIII Eagle Rolls-Royce engine arrived. It was a remarkable machine, for it had a large petrol tank slung under the fuselage with a view to giving it a greater petrol capacity and longer flying range. This tank, however, was not a success, but deserves mention as perhaps the finest piece of plumbing done by the Aircraft Depot concerned. This machine earned the name of P.P., which might have stood for Pouter Pigeon, owing to the appearance the tank gave the machine, had it not had a more strange and subtle significance which the Official Secrets Act forbids disclosing. The machines were in any case now fitted with an extra petrol tank under the pilot's seat, and this gave them a flying range of five and a half hours.

It is remarkable, when all things are considered, that there were not more crashes on Tantonville aerodrome than there were, for it was by no means an easy aerodrome to get into at the best of times, and at the end of a continuous flight of five hours or more, with the pleasantries of aerial warfare thrown in, any pilot could be excused "throwing his machine on the ground," as if to say, "And that's that!" In fact, not a few did.

Spring was now making itself felt, and the cat in the Technical Stores produced four very charming kittens, while the Squadron poet (?) produced a series of verses of a topical nature which went to a popular air from "Yes, Uncle," and became a nightly feature in the Mess, and, it is alleged, drove many to drink.

On St. George's Day a De Havilland 9 appeared on the aerodrome, the forerunner of a squadron which was due to arrive in May.

May, 1918.

May began with a comfortable show on the 2nd. On the afternoon of the same day an investiture was held by General de Castelnau, who decorated two pilots and two observers with the Croix de Guerre.

Part of the topical verse on this occasion ran as follows :—

We all of us saw, to our very great joy.
Each one of them kissed—and they did look so coy—
And we think the French General's a jolly old boy.
Really ? Yes ! Would you believe it ?

Thionville again was the objective on the 3rd ; then rainy weather held sway.

On the 6th there was some excitement caused by the escape of a German from a neighbouring prisoners-of-war camp.

So of course 55, each man taking a gun
Went off in two tenders to look for the Hun.
If only they'd found him, there would have been fun !

Thionville, for the third time in succession, was bombed on the 15th, followed by Saarbrucken on the 16th and Metz-Sablons on the 17th.

Then came a star show on the 18th, when Cologne was reached, the leader being a Flight Commander who had been invested on the 2nd with the Croix de Guerre.

Every one was very delighted with this raid, which made a Squadron record for distance flown there and back.

On Whit-Sunday the Recording Officer, who had been with the Squadron for nearly eighteen months, left for other parts. The Squadron was given a holiday on the strength of the good work of the day before.

Whit-Monday supplied a raid on Landau, Tuesday, the 21st, others on Namur and Charleroi, and the next day one on Liège. The lines were crossed at Verdun on the last three shows mentioned.

On the afternoon of the 22nd General Sir Hugh Trenchard paid a visit to the Squadron.

During the month the new squadron referred to in April had arrived and was ready for the fray. This was No. 99 Squadron, who were flying D.H.9's, and on Whit-Tuesday they began operations by a successful raid on Metz-Sablons.

The aerodrome was almost too small for two squadrons, but the overcrowding was not to last long, according to rumours that were going round.

The Officer Commanding 99 Squadron proved to be an old friend of 55's, having been in command of 57 Squadron, which had been a next-door neighbour both at Fienvillers and Boisdinghem.

On the 29th and 30th Thionville again

received attention, and the month ended with a good raid on Karlsruhe, on which more than a ton of explosives was dropped.

The total weight of bombs dropped during the month was 29,422 lbs., the highest figure up to date.

Amongst the twenty reconnaissances done during the month, other than numbered areas, were one on the 29th to Ludwigshafen and one on the 31st to Mannheim—flights of one hundred miles each way and done by solo machines.

June, 1918.

June operations opened on the 1st with a raid on the station at Conz, followed on the 3rd by one to Luxembourg, and on the 4th by others to Trèves and Conz.

On the 4th also the Squadron moved to Azelot, about fifteen miles distant by road, and nearer Nancy.

Azelot.

The first raid from the new aerodrome was to Coblenz on the 6th, then on successive days to Conz and Thionville.

On the 6th of June General Sir Hugh Trenchard was appointed to take command of the units operating under 8th Brigade, and the name of "Independent Force, R.A.F." was assumed.

On the 13th Trèves was the target, and then followed a spell of bad weather.

During this interval a communication was received by the Squadron, through Headquarters, 41st Wing, that read as follows:—

EXTRACT FROM LETTER FROM LE GÉNÉRAL DE DIVISION DE CASTELNAU, COMMANDANT DE L'EST.

Juin 7, 1918.

"Les services précieux que l'Aviation Anglaise de la région de l'Est a déjà rendu au G.E.A., sont un gage certain de l'aide qu'elle lui fournira dans l'avenir. Et à de sujet je tiens à vous signaler la façon particulièrement brillante dont se sont comportés jusqu'ici les unites de la 8e Brigade d'Aviation Britannique et en particulier le Squadron 55."

This was tantamount to a citation, but owing to a G.H.Q. ruling, could not be claimed as such. Nevertheless the Squadron was justly proud of the incident.

Operations commenced again on the 23rd with a raid on Metz-Sablons, repeated the next day, in addition to one on Dillingen.

Saarbruck followed on the 25th, and Karlsruhe on the 26th.

Thionville, once again, was visited on the 27th, and the month finished with bombs

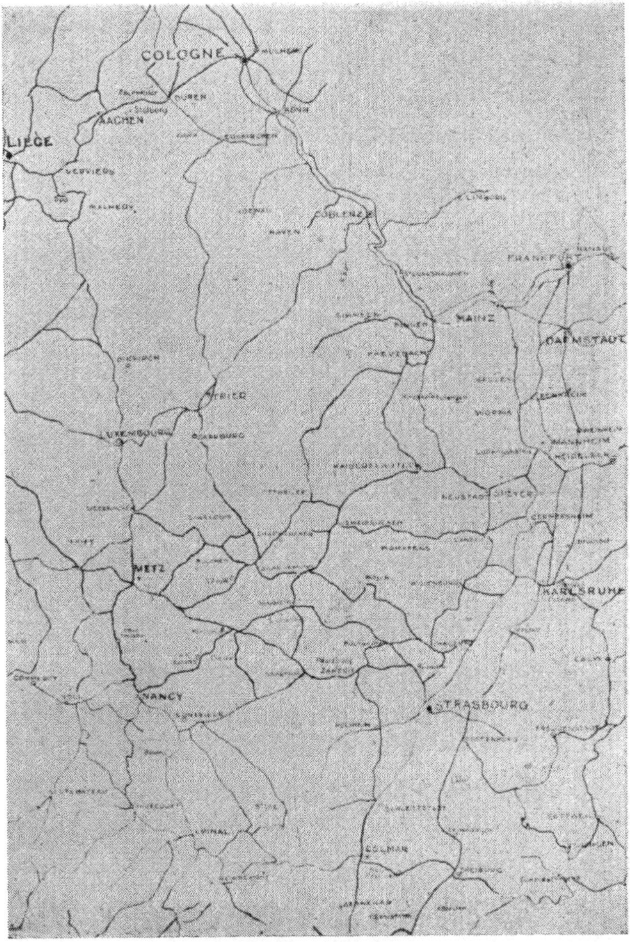

MAP OF "I.F." AREA.

dropped on Mannheim on the 29th and on Hagenau aerodrome on the 30th, bringing the total weight dropped up to 32,792 lbs.

Of the nine reconnaissances carried out, the majority were on the areas of St. Avold, Pfalzburg, and Frescaty.

On arrival at Azelot the Squadron found as its neighbour a new squadron, No. 104, who began work on the 8th of June with a useful raid to Metz-Sablons. Like 99, they too, flew the D.H.9.

99 followed 55 from Tantonville to Azelot early in the month.

The move to Azelot was appreciated by the majority of the pilots and observers, owing to the aerodrome's proximity to Nancy.

In the evenings, on an average of at least once a week, officers from the squadrons in the area made Nancy their rendezvous, and here fraternized with Americans and French, who likewise made full use of such opportunities for amusement as the place afforded.

Sometimes these evenings proved extremely lively; indeed, on one memorable occasion ....

.... DELETED BY CENSOR ....

....

which can easily be imagined.

July, 1918.

Early in July a "Croix Rouge" Hut was opened in the village of Azelot. This enterprise was in the hands of two English ladies, who did all that was possible for the men of the Squadron, by whom full use of the hut and its comforts was made.

Here was a pleasant reading-room, a well-stocked lending library, and a canteen, at which the ladies presided. On several occasions the Hut was used for squadron concerts, and every time was packed.

To the ladies concerned the thanks of 55 Squadron are due for the benefits derived from this Recreation Hut under their management, as is also a mark of admiration for their pluck in putting up with Hun bomb-raids and the other minor inconveniences of life in a war area.

For a while the Mess was honoured by their presence, but once the Hut was in full swing their duties prevented them from making use of such facilities as the Mess and ante-room afforded.

Wherever "Hands across the Sea" is heard, memory will recall the ladies of the "Croix Rouge" Hut at Azelot.

About this time the Hun started to

bombard Dombasle, about five miles away, and there was some discussion and speculation as to whether the aerodrome itself could be reached by his long-range guns, or whether the intervening hills came in the way of the trajectory of the shells. However, nothing of the kind happened, the only ill-results to the Squadron being to find itself suddenly very unpopular with the French at Dombasle and St. Nicolas, who declared, rumour said, that the bombardment was a reprisal for the Squadron's bomb raids.

Friendly feeling, however, was soon restored after the French had put the gun out of action.

The opening raid in July was on the railways and workshops at Conz and Trèves on the 1st.

On the 2nd Coblenz received its third visit, followed by a fourth on the 5th.

The 6th supplied a short show to Metz-Sablons.

On the 7th only a reconnaissance was sent out, and that to Boulay aerodrome and area.

As was expected, the Hun soon discovered that Azelot aerodrome was occupied by three squadrons, all of whom were distinctly troublesome during the day, so he retaliated by a little night-bombing. At first he flew over but dropped nothing; not that the effect on morale was much lessened thereby, for waiting for it is often as bad as the reality.

However, on the night of Sunday, the 7th, he dropped his first bomb on the aerodrome, destroying 104 Squadron's transport shed and slightly damaging some of the vehicles.

On the same afternoon the Squadron had held some very successful sports, followed by a concert in the evening in the Croix Rouge Hut.

Next day Luxembourg was the objective.

A new arrival in the Squadron in the form of an American-built D.H.4 with a Liberty engine caused great interest and much speculation as to how it would compare with the D.H.4's fitted with the VIII Eagle Rolls-Royce used on reconnaissances.

On the 11th a raid was made on Offenburg, on the 12th to Saarburg, and then again to Offenburg on the 15th.

Thionville followed on the 16th and 17th, and the munition works at Oberndorf on the 20th.

On the 22nd the powder factories at Rottwell were successfully attacked, on the 30th Offenburg, and on the 31st Coblenz, totalling 32,792 lbs. of bombs for the month.

Perhaps it should be stated that for brevity's sake the town alone is named as the objective; it must be borne in mind that the target ordered to be bombed was always some special point of a military nature.

The photographic reconnaissances for the month of July, nine in number, were confined to the areas around Hun aerodromes, amongst which Boulay (Bolchen) predominated.

August, 1918.

During the summer months motoring in the neighbourhood of Azelot was very pleasant, and as certain duty journeys had to be performed by the transport, advantage was often taken of spare seats on tenders by officers wishing to see the country and enjoy the scenery.

The majority of runs took one into the department of the Vosges, either to Charmes or Chatenois, near Neufchateau; the former was a depot for rations and also the site of the hospital, so the journeys there were not always enjoyable. Chatenois was the location of the Pilots' Pool and another source of supply for the Mess, there being an Expeditionary Force Canteen in the town.

At Vezelise the Aircraft Park had its being (its " doings " must be told elsewhere). The traffic to and fro was great, for from here came all stores of a technical nature, and supplies such as petrol, oils, and bombs. Tantonville, famous for its beer, was near by. On the road there one could study quite a variety of nations. Leaving Azelot, one probably passed an Indian Labour Corps at work, near Flavigny Italians could be seen, in the village of Ceintrey were Russians, while near by was an encampment of Algerian road-menders, and before reaching Vezelise a few Cochin Chinese troops might be met planting telegraph poles.

The best sight-seeing trips fell, however, to breakdown parties fetching in machines that had forced-landed and crashed. In such cases lorries and trailers penetrated into the departments of Haute Marne, Haute Saône, and even Doubs ; the last-named being contiguous to Switzerland.

On the whole, if one likes variety of scenery there are few opportunities of seeing it cheaply better than those afforded to a Mechanical Transport driver in the R.A.F. overseas.

For some time now the Squadron had had attached to it American pilots from the "American Air Service Units with the British Expeditionary Force," and of the qualities of these, both as pilots and comrades, the Squadron registers a great appreciation.

In addition to those who were of the A.A.S.R.C. were also those who had joined the R.F.C. in Canada, and were content to merge their nationality, temporarily, and serve in His Majesty's Forces. To the combination of these the Squadron is indebted for its introduction to the "Ukulele," and the strains of this instrument from far-away Hawaii charmed alike the pilots and observers after a hard day's work; as much, too, as it pleased the Chinese Labour Corps, members of which worked about the aerodrome and camp and stole one's safety razors.

As at Fienvillers, the Squadron's camp was in an orchard, so too was it at Azelot.

August opened with a raid on Düren on the 1st, followed by bad weather until the 8th, when Rombas was the objective.

Buhl aerodrome and Metz-Sablons were bombed on the 11th.

The next day, under skilful leadership, Frankfort-on-Main was reached, an objective about 135 miles away from the aerodrome.

The following days Buhl and Offenburg were the targets, and then again on the 16th another long-distance raid about equal in distance to that on the 12th was made to Darmstadt under the same leadership.

On the return of the raid on Buhl aerodrome on the 13th a Hun machine was shot down on this side of the lines, which was unusual, for it very rarely happened that hostile aircraft would follow a formation across the lines.

This machine was shot down in flames, and, though the wreckage was claimed and handed over to the Squadron, there was very little of it left unspoiled either by fire or the subsequent crash to earth.

However, on a metal tubular strut it was possible to read " Fok. D.7 (OAW) 4461/18," which was interesting, inasmuch as it disclosed the type of the machine and the date of building.

The engine was a six-cylinder vertical Mercédès (?). The name-plate, however, had been removed by some souvenir-hunter. The propeller was stamped " Axial."

On the 14th, again, a solitary Hun followed one of our machines, which was in difficulties and forced to land, down to earth.

The Hun imagined that he had made a safe capture, and landed near by, and crashed. He was somewhat annoyed to find that he had landed on the wrong side of the lines, however, and was, instead of a captor, a captive, for the French troops took prompt action on his crashing and incidentally retained the machine, which 55 considered belonged to them.

During the week the photographic machines were very busy on the areas of Strasbourg, and Morhange, Boulay and Hagenau.

On the 22nd Coblenz and Wittlich were bombed.

The following day Trèves received a visit.

Morhange aerodrome and Luxembourg were the targets for the 25th, and Conflans on the 27th, followed by Thionville and Conflans again on the 30th, to finish the month up.

August was rather severe in casualties, unfortunately, for seven pilots and observers were missing, one pilot and observer killed, two observers died of wounds, and one pilot and two observers were wounded. For the raid on the 23rd three observers were lent by 99 Squadron.

On the night of the 30th the Hun made his first really serious bomb raid on the Squadron's living quarters, coming over about nine in the evening and catching everybody unawares. A parachute flare was dropped, and the "Archie" battery on the hill as well as the camps of 55 and 104 Squadrons were the recipients of a number of heavy bombs.

Beyond minor damages, 55 got off lightly; 104 unluckily sustained several casualties to personnel.

One bomb came down in the field alongside 55's orchard and in a line with the Officers' Mess, in which a number of pilots and observers were gathered. Luckily it was a "dud." Next day it was dug up by the Armament Officer and emptied, and, having been slung up outside the ante-room, fulfilled the function of a raid-warning gong thereafter.

September, 1918.

The month began with great activity in the Flight Hangars and Headquarters Workshops in connection with the installation of VIII Eagle Rolls-Royce engines in every machine in place of VI and VII Eagles.

On the 2nd the Squadron was bombed again, but with only slight damage and with one minor casualty.

Buhl aerodrome had that day had its turn from the Squadron; it had it again on the 4th.

On the 6th some excitement was caused by a Hun Hannover biplane, a two-seater with Opel engine, attempting to land on the aerodrome. "Archie" opened up from the hill and frightened it away, and French Spads went up after it. The Huns eventually landed and were captured, and the machine was exhibited in the Place Stanislas, Nancy, on the following Sunday.

While engaged on a photographic reconnaissance on the 7th the special "Jumbo" ran into trouble and was so badly shot about that it had to be written off. This machine was the only D.H.4.A that the Squadron ever possessed, and was peculiar in that it had large surface planes, similar to those on the D.H.9.A, but in other respects it was the same as the normal D.H.4's fitted with VIII Eagle Rolls-Royce engines.

On the same day and on the 14th the railways at Ehrange were attacked, while on the 15th the Daimler works at Stuttgart and on the 16th the Lanz works at Mannheim were the objectives.

The Squadron Commander left, and was succeeded as Commanding Officer by the Flight Commander who led the Frankfort and Darmstadt raids.

About this time a new-comer was to be seen on the aerodrome in the shape of the D.H.10 belonging to 104 Squadron, a machine fitted with two Liberty engines.

The raid on the 25th was on the munition factories at Kaiserslautern, and the last of the month, on the 26th, on the railways at Audun-le-Roman.

Seventeen reconnaissances were done during the month, some of which were in connection with the St. Mihiel salient attack made by the American troops.

September, too, had witnessed the debut of another squadron, No. 110, who flew D.H.9.A's fitted with Liberty engines. On the 14th they started work by dropping 2,028 lbs. of bombs upon Boulay aerodrome.

Visitors from French squadrons or American squadrons flying French machines were often to be seen on the aerodrome. Amongst

MANNHEIM.

[From a water-colour by LIEUT. BERTRAM SANDY.]

By permission of the Imperial War Museum.

the most interesting were a two-engined Caudron, a Bréguet two-seater, and a Salmson two-seater.

A spectacular visitor was a Handley-Page which landed in a hurry downwind, nearly charged a hangar, wheeled sharply round, taxied down the aerodrome, and burst into flames all around her starboard engine.

The Ambulance tender with 55's fire picquet was promptly on the scene, together with various other people, and the fire was put out, but the Handley-Page remained a fortnight or so a sorry sight, until, having been leisurely dismantled, her last remains were removed by road to whence she came.

October, 1918.

October proved a month of bad weather.

However, on the 15th, in spite of rain, a D.H.4 left the ground and bombed the aerodrome at Frescaty from 150 feet. The pilot made use of the low-lying clouds and his speed very cleverly, and had come and gone almost before the Huns knew he was there. For this excellent effort he was awarded the D.F.C., which came through two days later.

Incidentally, this same pilot had been

the reserve on the show on Easter Day, 1917. He had been invalided home later, and had recently returned to the Squadron.

The next raid was not until the 21st, and then was upon Thionville. It was followed by another on the 23rd upon Metz-Sablons.

Another spell of impossible weather followed, but on the 29th Longuyon was bombed.

The month finished well with raids on the 31st upon Frescaty, Trèves, and Bonn; the last-named being the last long-distance raid the Squadron did, and was little short in distance of that on Cologne.

On the 30th October the Huns paid a visit to the neighbourhood, but failed to find the aerodrome owing to the thick white ground mist.

During the month No. 45 Squadron had arrived from Italy and were flying Sopwith Camels. They began work on the 23rd, and before the month had ended had accounted for two Hun machines.

November, 1918.

The month opened with a raid on Saarburg on the 3rd. On the 6th two raids set out, one to Attigny, the other to Burbach. The last-named raid proved a very "hot show" indeed, for the formation was attacked by hostile aircraft in superior numbers of four to one. Though unfortunately one D.H.4 was lost, the Huns paid for it with four of theirs.

One experienced observer was heard to declare that it was the worst show he had been on, and to the onlooker it was obvious, on seeing all the pilots and observers concerned on their return, that they must have gone through a very nerve-racking time.

On the 9th Bensdorf was bombed, and on the 10th the railways at Ehrange.

The following day hostilities ceased.

In spite of the few raids done in the month two pilots and observers were missing and the like number killed.

Of the two machines missing, one was that of the pilot who had done the solo raid on Frescaty in October. From his observer, who got back again after the Armistice, it was learnt that the machine had been hit by "Archie," severely wounding the pilot, who, unhappily, succumbed to his injuries. The observer landed the machine and, fortunately, escaped unhurt.

A week later the Squadron packed up

and left. The machines made an excellent flight from Azelot to Le Planly aerodrome.

Le Planly.

The transport came up by road without a hitch, and the personnel and other impedimenta came by train to Auxi-le-Chateau.

During the move from Azelot to Le Planly the Squadron lost Roger. He left the train to stretch his legs along with many another, and, sad as it is to relate, the train started suddenly and left him behind. He was last seen trying to catch the train up. In any case it was a vain quest, for he could not have leapt in, so he stayed behind in the Province of Champagne. Rumour has it that he died of a broken heart. It may have been grief; it may have been disgust at having failed to overtake a French train. But whatever his fate, his memory remains, and the name of Pol Roger will ever be connected with Champagne.

Poor old Roger dog!

On the 24th the Commanding Officer and the Equipment Officer, arriving back from duty in England, found everything done for them, a matter which met with their fullest approval.

The stay at Le Planly proved very short, and at the end of the month preparations were afoot for another move.

December, 1918.
St. André-aux-Bois.

On December 2nd the Squadron moved to St. André-aux-Bois, near Hesdin, and on the 5th began mail-carrying work, the first delivery being to Mons.

This work was carried on intermittently till the end of the month, as far as weather conditions would allow.

Christmas was spent happily, in spite of the mud-bound condition of the camp.

During the afternoon of Christmas Day the Mechanical Transport kindly afforded an entertainment by setting their office on fire. Great heroism was displayed on all sides, but the aim of certain persons with fire extinguishers could have been improved upon, for some must have been extinguishing a fire on a neighbouring shed, visible only to themselves.

A Christmas dinner of a large and varied order ensued ; the waiting was excellent.

To wind up the evening the Mechanical Transport again, assisted by "a lady of unlimited allurements" and others, supplied a show which was much appreciated.

The rest of the evening was in accordance with Christmas custom. There were no casualties.

To echo the sentiments expressed at the end of the Christmas show, a word is due in praise of the men of the Squadron for their *esprit de corps* at all times and for their capacity for working hard and working well, since, thanks to their share in the "Per Ardua," were possible the results by which pilots and observers carried the name of the Squadron "ad Astra" between March, 1917, and November, 1918.

January, 1919.

With the New Year things moved rapidly, and during the month of January the machines and stores were handed over and the personnel passed to Reinforcement Parks, and are now either demobilized or else in other squadrons of the Army of Occupation.

By the end of the month the Squadron, now reduced to cadre—a shadow of its former self—proceeded to Renfrew in Scotland, and France knew it no more.

Such was the anti-climax caused by the Armistice.

O mighty Squadron! dost thou leave France so?
Are all thy conquests, glories, triumphs, spoils,
Shrunk to this little measure?—Fare thee well.

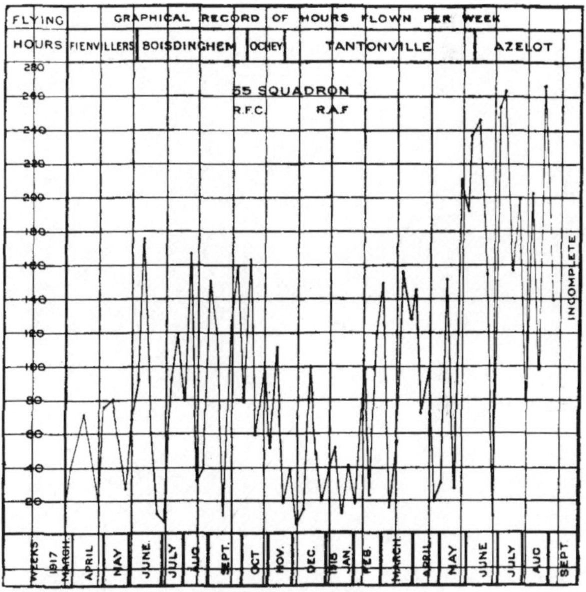

7,000 HOURS CHART.

EPILOGUE

So far our paths have been the same, but here we part, each bearing with him the memories of happy strenuous days.

Of "55" we shall ever think and speak with real affection and no little pride, and some may even sigh, regretting it has ceased to be.

It surely is not to Our Country's good that the Squadron, so vital and so keen, the possessor of traditions worthy of posterity, should have blossomed and then have been let fade.

But, though it cannot bloom again, the fragrance of its memories is yours and mine to keep.

And now, Good-bye and may Good Luck attend you.

YOUR CHRONICLER.

"Thus far, with rough and all-unable pen,
  Our bending author hath pursued his story;
In little room confining mighty men,
  Mangling by starts the full course of their glory."

Henry V.

APPENDIX I

DECORATIONS

D.S.O.

Capt. W. B. Farrington.

M.C.

Lieut. P. J. Barnett.
Lieut. R. de R. Brett.
Capt. J. M. Burd.
Capt. J. B. Fox.
Capt. A. Gray.
Lieut. A. S. Keep.
Capt. E. A. B. Rice.
Capt. B. J. Silly.
Capt. C. A. Stevens.
Capt. F. M. C. Turner.
Lieut. H. S. P. Walmsley.
Capt. F. Williams.

Croix de Guerre.

Lieut. C. A. Bridgland.
Lieut. J. M. Carroll.
Capt. S. B. Collett.
Capt. W. B. Farrington, D.S.O.
Capt. A. Gray, M.C.
Lieut. C. D. Palmer.
Capt. R. P. Ward, M.C.
Lieut. E. J. Whyte, D.F.C.
Lieut. W. Wild.
Capt. F. Williams, M.C.

Bar to M.C.

Lieut. S. S. Jones, M.C.
Capt. C. A. Stevens, M.C.

D.F.C.

Capt. O. L. Beater.
Capt. J. R. Bell.
Lieut. C. L. Heater, U.S.A.
Capt. D. R. G. Mackay.
Lieut. W. J. Pace.
Lieut. J. Parke.
Lieut. W. R. Patey.
Lieut. C. L. Rayment.
Capt. B. J. Silly, M.C.
Lieut. E. R. Stewart.
Lieut. E. F. Van der Riet.
Capt. R. P. Ward, M.C.
Lieut. D. J. Waterous.
Lieut. P. E. Welchman, M.C.
Lieut. E. J. Whyte.
Capt. F. Williams, M.C.

Ordre de la Couronne.

Major J. E. A. Baldwin.

Croix de Guerre (Belgium).

Major J. E. A. Baldwin.
Lieut. R. W. Rose.

M.M.

Sergt. Allan.
A.M. Ellis.
Pte. Fraser.
A.M. Leyland.
Sergt. Moreman.
Cpl. Walters.

D.F.M.

Sergt. Clare.

Medaille Militaire.

Sergt. Allan.
Sergt. Howard.

Médaille d'Honneur.

A.M. Taylor.

M.S.M.

C.M.M. Cummins.
F.-Sergt. Parsons.
F.-Sergt. Redpath.
F.-Sergt. Robinson.

Bronze Medal for Valour (Italian).

Sergt. Ryan.

Decoration Militaire (Belgian).

A.M. Tibbles.

Mentioned in Dispatches.

Lt.-Col. J. E. A. Baldwin, D.S.O.
Major A. Gray, M.C.
Lieut. N. H. Thackrah.

(*Subject to additions and corrections.*)

APPENDIX II

R.F.C. 55 SQUADRON R.A.F.

MARCH, 1917, TO NOVEMBER, 1918.

Officers Commanding.

Major J. E. A. Baldwin, D.S.O.
Major A. Gray, M.C.
Major B. J. Silly, M.C., D.F.C.

Equipment Officers.

2nd-Lieut. D. Drover.
Lieut. L. Miller.

Armament Officers.

2nd-Lieut. W. H. M. Groom.
Lieut. C. B. Harris.

Recording Officers.

Capt. E. E. Colquhoun.
Capt. A. B. Mitchell.
Lieut. F. Allen.
Lieut. F. Nixon.

Flight Commanders.

Capt. E. A. B. Rice, M.C.
Capt. D. A. Davidson, M.C.
Capt. Thayre.
Capt. F. S. Moller, M.C.
Capt. A. B. Adams.
Capt. I. V. Pyott, D.S.O.
Capt. F. M. C. Turner, M.C.
Capt. A. Gray, M.C.
Capt. C. A. Stevens, M.C.
Capt. J. M. Burd, M.C.
Capt. B. J. Silly, M.C., D.F.C.
Capt. J. B. Fox, M.C.
Capt. W. B. Farrington, D.S.O.

Flight Commanders.

Capt. S. B. Collett.
Capt. F. Williams, M.C., D.F.C.
Capt. H. S. P. Walmsley, M.C.
Capt. J. R. Bell, D.F.C.
Capt. D. R. G. Mackay, D.F.C.
Capt. W. J. Pace, D.F.C.

Attached Officers.

Photographic—Capt. B. F. Crane.
Meteorological—Capt. W. F. G. Brunt.
Intelligence—Capt. A. Lloyd, M.B.E.
Intelligence—Capt. A. R. Ovens, M.B.E.
Medical Officer—Capt. H. Gardiner-Hill, M.B.E.

Chaplains.

Capt. P. H. Wilson, C.F.
Capt. Berry, C.F.

APPENDIX III

MACHINE AND ENGINE USED EXCLUSIVELY

De Havilland 4.

Two-seater biplane, designed and constructed by Aircraft Manufacturing Co., Hendon.

Others built by :—

Westland Aircraft Co., Yeovil.

Palladium Autocars, Putney, S.W.

(A, B, D and F Series.)

Note.—The American-built D.H.4 referred to in July, 1918, No. 32077, constructed by Dayton-Wright Aircraft Co., Dayton, Ohio, U.S.A., fitted with 400-h.p., 12-cylinder Liberty engine.

Rolls-Royce.

Designed and built by :—

Rolls-Royce, Ltd., Derby.

Eagle Series I to VIII, 12 cylinder, 4½ inches bore and 6½ inches stroke, ranging from 250 h.p. to 350 h.p.

Watford Magnetos.

Lodge Sparking Plugs.

NOTES

GENERAL OFFICER COMMANDING 8TH BRIGADE :—
Brig.-Gen. C. L. N. Newall, C.M.G., A.M.

OFFICER COMMANDING 9TH WING :—
Lieut.-Col. C. L. N. Newall, A.M.

OFFICERS COMMANDING 41ST WING :—
Lieut.-Col. C. L. N. Newall, A.M.
Lieut.-Col. J. E. A. Baldwin, D.S.O.
Lieut.-Col. L. A. Pattison, M.C., D.F.C.

8-4-17.—Casualties :—
Capt. Logan.
Lieuts. Henry, Evans, White, Hamar, and Myberg.

28-4-17.—Reference to :—
Capt. Moller, M.C.

4-5-17.—Congratulations on work of Lieuts. Turner and Brett.

10-5-17.—Casualties :—
Lieuts. Pitt and Holroyde (the latter shot down a Hun even while his own machine was going down in flames).

11-6-17.—Decoration :—
Capt. E. A. B. Rice.

2-7-17.—Reference to :—
2nd-Lieut. B. F. Sandy.

22-7-17.—Reference to :—
Lieuts. Knight and Trulock.

16-8-17.—Reference to :—
Lieut. Waters.

August, 1917.—What about the "Observers' Union"?

?–9–17.—BRUSSELS.—Brussels reconnaissance accomplished by:—

Lieuts. Loyd and Deason.

11–10–17.—BOISDINGHEM-OCHEY.—Pilots of machines concerned:—

Capts. Gray, Burd, and Farrington.
Lieuts. Walmsley and Thackrah.

17–10–17.—BURBACH.—Leaders of Raid:—

Capt. J. M. Burd and Capt. W. B. Farrington.

October, 1917.—Capt. Davis, of the R.A.S.C.

5–12–17.—SAARBRÜCK.

"Saarbrück was attacked at 2.25 p.m. on December 5th, 1917. About eleven bombs were dropped. A house and drug-store were seriously damaged. Two bombs fell near a repair shop in Saarbrück Station, damaging telegraph and telephone wires."

(*Extract from Report.*)

24–12–17.—MANNHEIM.—Leaders of Raid:—

Capt. Stevens, M.C., and Capt. W. B. Farrington.

Missing:—

Lieuts. Turner and Castle.

January, 1918.—Major Gray, M.C., succeeded Major Baldwin as O.C. Squadron.

19–2–18.—TRÈVES.—Lieuts. Ross and Hewitt missing.

10–3–18.—Capt. J. B. Fox, M.C., and Lieut. S. S. Jones, M.C., replaced on reconnaissance by Capt. Collett and Lieut. J. Parke.

10–3–18.—STUTTGART.—Lieuts. Caldecott and Thomas missing.

12-3-18.—COBLENZ.—Leader of Raid:—
Capt. W. B. Farrington.

13-3-18.—FREIBURG.—Lieuts. Wilson, Gavaghan, Brookes, and Cann missing.

12-3-18.—COBLENZ.

"One bomb exploded in the Barracks amongst a company lined up to receive their meals. Four soldiers were killed and twelve wounded."

(*Extract from Report.*)

24-3-18.—Below is a contribution by "Bumps" to 55's Chronicles. In the letter which came with it he says: "I've left out the scrap with eight Huns; you would not want that. It was not too pleasant with 'Tony' out of ammunition."

Here is what he says:—

"The following is a rough sketch of what happened to me in Hunland:—

"We crashed close to Düss, and were immediately surrounded by Infantry, civilians, etc., and so could not fire the machine. First we were taken into an Artillery Officers' Mess for lunch, then to a car with Press photographers in attendance, and so to the Headquarters at Düss.

"Here we were questioned separately, and afterwards Fluke was put into a shed, and I was put into a cottage where Hun soldiers were billeted. These were quite decent fellows, and gave me coffee and beer. Whilst here, several of the civilian population came to have a chat—probably after information.

" About 9 o'clock that evening we were taken to the station and after changing twice, and spending most of the night in a village waiting-room, where we were even refused a drink of water, we arrived at St. Avold.

" After walking about two miles, we reached Headquarters, where we were separated again and questioned. We were then put in solitary confinement in the barracks for eleven days on ordinary Hun soldiers' rations.

" At the end of this time we started off together for Karlsruhe, and arrived there on April 3rd. We spent the night in the hotel, which is well known by all prisoners. The next morning we were taken down separately and questioned. Here they very kindly told us our Squadron Commander's name, our Wing Commander's name, and our Brigade Commander's name, although neither of us had any papers in our possession when we were captured, nor had we spoken to each other about the Squadron.

" The next day we were taken into the Camp and searched, then allowed to join the other prisoners. After this we were permitted to send telegrams home through Switzerland.

" We saw Wilson, who had been wounded, but was practically all right again. After three or four days about thirty of us were sent to Landshut.

" Here is a tiny little camp. Twenty-two of us had to sleep in one small room, while a piece of ground about the same size as a tennis-court was all we had for exercise. Every day we were shut in at 6 p.m.

"While here we were inoculated five times, also vaccinated, and our clothes were thoroughly searched.

"After about five weeks we were sent to Holzminden. On the journey we were quite well treated, but they took every precaution against our escape.

"On arrival at the Camp, the Commandant, the notorious Captain Niemeyer, welcomed us with his time-honoured 'joke' that he wanted forty-eight hours' notice if any of us intended to escape.

"In this Camp there were fifteen of 55 Squadron :—Henry, Ross, Hewitt, Turner, Castle, Caldecott, Thomas, Wilson, Webster, Adamson, Waters, Fluke, O'Lieff, Wells, and myself.

"From then it was simply a case of waiting until the Armistice was signed.

"N. H. T."

24-3-18.—Casualty : Sergeant Ryan.

April, 1918.—By special request a few verses have been inserted at the end of the Notes.

16-5-18.—KAISERSLAUTERN.—2nd-Lieut. R. C. Sansom missing.

17-5-18.—METZ-SABLONS.—Twelve De Havilland 4's of 55 Squadron bombed the railway station and sidings at Metz. Twenty-four 112-lb. bombs were dropped from 14,000 ft., and some very good bursts were observed. Twenty-one plates were exposed, and the photographs show excellent shooting. All machines returned safely.

The pilots concerned were Capt. Farrington, Lieuts. Whyte, Bell, Whitelock, Walmsley, and MacIntyre.

Capt. Collett, Lieuts. Waterous, Pace, Godet, Jones, M.C., and Townsend.

Extract from Report of Raid on METZ main station, showing damage done and loss of life incurred, including a "near thing":—

"Between 4.35 and 4.50 p.m. twelve machines attacked the main station and railway triangle of Metz-Sablons. Several bombs were dropped. Five bombs fell on the main station, one between tracks No. 4 and 5 alongside a stationary express train. Bombs also fell in the station square and on several other tracks and goods sheds. The loss of life incurred was great. It appears that some high General was expected, and a guard of honour of both mounted and dismounted men had been drawn up. In the train itself eleven military officers were killed and forty-six other ranks severely wounded. Several horses were killed, while in the station itself thirty odd men were killed and wounded, . . . it appears that the "high General" was the Kaiser himself! He, however, did not come to Metz, as his train was held up at Thionville, and he was taken to the Château near Florange."

18-5-18.—COLOGNE.

"Forty-three persons were killed and fifty-five injured, some of them seriously. Serious damage was done to thirty-eight buildings. According to present estimates material damage to the extent of 340,000 marks was caused."

18-5-18.—COLOGNE.—Pilots concerned: Capt. F. Williams, Lieuts. Walmsley, Bell, Reynolds, Wild, and Keep.

MESSAGES received by Officer Commanding 55 Squadron through 8th Brigade:—

(1) "Splendid. Am coming to see you shortly. Give my congratulations to all pilots and observers.

"MAJOR-GENERAL TRENCHARD."

(2) "Very best congratulations to 8th Brigade and No. 55 Squadron on the successful bombing of Cologne to-day.

"GENERAL SALMOND."

19-5-18.—Refers to our old friend "Coote," now an M.B.E.

May, 1917.—O.C. 99 Squadron, Major L. A. Pattison, M.C., afterwards O.C., 41st Wing.

31-5-18.—KARLSRUHE.—Pilots concerned:—

Capt. F. Williams, Lieutenants Legge, MacIntyre, Clarke, Van der Riet, and Anderson.

O.C. 104 Squadron, Major J. C. Quinnell (afterwards O.C. 49 Squadron).

Croix Rouge Hut:—Mrs. Huntington and Miss Studholme.

16-7-18.—THIONVILLE.

"Twenty bombs dropped in the station. A munition train received two direct hits, and fifteen trucks at once exploded and caught fire. Shells contained in the trucks exploded at intervals. The remaining twenty-five trucks were detached and brought to a place of safety. An additional five trucks which were stationary in the loading sidings also exploded, as well as one truck of small-arm ammunition.

" Exploding shells set fire to the express goods shed. The fire spread to the goods despatch buildings and other trucks near goods shed and sidings; a conflagration resulted.

" In another building loose shells stacked in heaps exploded, and two other buildings containing hand grenades and small-arm ammunition were exploded and burnt out. Near the main munition train a horse transport train was standing. In addition to horses, it contained medical comforts, straw, forage and rations. Sixty horses were killed or seriously wounded.

" Despite the co-operation of two motor fire-engines, it was impossible to save trucks or buildings, which were left to burn themselves out.

" In all, five locomotives were more or less seriously damaged, fifty trucks were burnt and another fifty partially destroyed.

" Rails for 200 metres were badly damaged and water mains from water towers destroyed. All traffic was stopped and telephonic communication cut off owing to damage to wires.

" Casualties in personnel totalled eighty-three German military killed or wounded, and ten civilians killed."

(*Extract from Report.*)

1-8-18.—DÜREN.

"The entire damage officially reported up to date (December, 1918) amounts to 170,561 marks."

(*Extract from Report.*)

12-8-18.—FRANKFORT-ON-MAIN.—Objective : Factories and Railways. Extracts from Official Report by Leader of Raid :—

Twelve D.H.4's left ground 5.20 a.m. Twelve machines reached objective at 8 a.m.

Anti-aircraft fire heavy, but very inaccurate.

Enemy aircraft activity considerable. About forty scouts of various types attacked formation from west of Mannheim, going to objective and on the return. One enemy machine was shot down in flames and seen to break up, another seen to crash into a wood, two others were driven down out of control, and one was driven down.

Bombs as follows were dropped from 14,000 feet : Two 230-lb., eighteen 112-lb., eight 25-lb., two 40-lb. (phosphorus), and eight plates were exposed.

Bursts in town east of goods station were observed.

LEADER.

Capt. B. J. Silly, M.C.	Capt. D. R. Mackay.
2nd-Lieut. W. R. Patey.	2nd-Lieut. H. C. T. Gompertz.
Lieut. J. Cunliffe.	Lieut. G. T. Richardson.
2nd-Lieut. J. E. Little.	2nd-Lieut. G. Madge.

LEADER.

2nd-Lieut. D. J. Waterous.[1]	Lieut. C. L. Heater, U.S.A.
2nd-Lieut. J. R. Fox.	Sergt. Allan.
2nd-Lieut. P. J. Cunningham.	Lieut. P. M. Payson, U.S.A.
2nd-Lieut. N. Wallace.	2nd-Lieut. J. A. Lee.
Lieut. P. E. Welchman, M.C.	Lieut. C. A. Bridgland.
Sergt. Clare.	2nd-Lieut. E. R. Stewart, D.F.C.[2]
Lieut. E. P. Critchley.	Lieut. S. L. Dowswell.
Sergt. Lewis.	2nd-Lieut. C. W. Clutson.

The lines were crossed at 11,000 feet over BADONVILLER, and a course was steered over PFALZBOURG, east of KAISERSLAUTERN, west of WORMS, GR. GERAU, to objective, where bombs were dropped from a height of 14,000 feet with excellent results. The same route was followed on the return journey.

On leaving the VOSGES, large numbers of enemy aircraft (mostly scouts) attacked our formations, but did not press the attack with much vigour, owing to our excellent formation.

One enemy aeroplane was seen to go down in flames and another crashed into a wood.

Weather conditions were exceedingly good, and there was practically no wind.

Duration of flight: 5 hours 29 minutes.

O.C. 110 Squadron.—Major H. R. Nicholl.

15-10-18.—Capt. D. R. G. Mackay.

[1] Photographic Machine. [2] Casualty: killed in action.

31–10–18.—BONN.—The day raid on BONN at 3.20 p.m. caused heavy casualties to the civilian population. It appears that the warning was received later than usual, and that at the time the streets were full of people. When the first bomb fell the people crowded together, and one bomb fell on a number of people who were waiting to get into a tram.

6–11–18.—BURBACH.—Lieut. Richardson pilot of missing machine.

2–12–18.—MONS mails first trip. Capt. J. B. Fox, M.C., Lieut. J. Parke, D.F.C.

TRANSFERS.

Capt. Davidson, M.C., to No. 19 Squadron.

Capt. Thayre to No. 20 Squadron.[1]

Capt. Adams to No. 1 Squadron (to be O.C.).

Lieut. Tempest, D.S.O., to No. 100 Squadron (afterwards O.C.).

Capt. Turner, M.C., to No. 57 Squadron.

The following officers went from 55 Squadron to be Flight Commanders in other Squadrons of the Independent Force :—

Capt. P. E. Welchman, M.C., D.F.C., 99 Squadron.

Capt. J. Cunliffe, 104 Squadron.

Capt. D. J. Waterous, D.F.C., 110 Squadron.

[1] 20 Squadron afterwards claimed to be the record Squadron of the R.F.C. and R.A.F., with a total bag of over six hundred Hun machines destroyed.

PERSONAL.

55 Squadron drew its members from all parts of the world, the following countries being represented :—

Great Britain and Ireland, Canada (all provinces), U.S.A., Bermuda, Falkland Islands, Malay States, India, Ceylon, South Africa, Egypt, Australia, New Zealand, Spain and Switzerland.

APOLOGIES.

It is regretted that the "Notes" are not of a more comprehensive nature, but on reference to the Officer Commanding the Cadre of 55, at Renfrew, a reply was received, of which the following is an extract :—

"Under the circumstances I do not think it necessary to wade through the records again for the information asked for."

THANKS.

However, the particulars that are given are from such records as it was possible to obtain access to, thanks to the courtesy of Major Paul, O.B.E., M.C., and the remainder from personal memoranda.

Acknowledgment is also due to Major Paul for his permission to use extracts from his Report on the Results of the Independent Force Bombing, over which bombing area he had personally toured, with Captain Ovens, M.B.E., visiting the various objectives and ascertaining the extent of the damage caused.

MISCELLANEA

ECHOES

Have you ever heard any one say ?—

" Stitski ! " " Perfectly amazing." " I simply sobbed with laughter." " La dee da da." " I'm different." " Gad's teeth ! " " Shee-ut up." " 'ullo, old bean." " Topping." " Shuggar." " Say—guy . . ." " Don't be a fool, you fool." " Priceless." " Chucklets." " . . . ! " " Wilt have a bun ? " " No, what ? " " What about a spot of . . . ? " " . . . a job of work." " Ha, ah ! " " Good morning." " . . . my regiment." " And what will the sailor sing ? " " You are a one ! "

Do you remember ?—

Count Titti de Hoogstadt, Fanny, Twitters, Coote, Bombs, Lloyd MK II, Daddy, Sticky, Bumps, Fifi, Van, Don, Tinkle, Mac, Beerjay, Alick, Johnbee, Jimmy, Gertie, Esses, Shingles, The Farrier, Oscar, Willy, Percy, Pip, Lady Di, Ikey, Briar, Bill, Tank, Rosie, Steve, Ah der Ah, Nobby, Dick, Reggie and the Little Man.

EXTRACTS FROM AN EXPURGATED GLOSSARY

Obtain.—A euphemism instituted by a very worthy Flight-Sergeant, who was alleged in a song to have come from the Isle of Man.
cf. " Scrounge, hot stuff."

To Commit Crashery.—A form of landing indulged in, after which the last state of the machine is worse than the first.

A Flat Spin.—The state of mind resulting when, having said " Rats," or the equivalent, into the telephone, you find the Brigadier is at the other end.

Eternity Tunic.—A R.F.C. tunic, which lasts for ever, in spite of A.M.W.O.'s urging that R.A.F. kit be worn.

Cant Hat.—A R.F.C. cap, so-called because it is worn on one side.

Split-Ace Merchant.—Split-half, as in splits=half sodas. Ace—star pilot. *cf.* French: " as."
Total=half-star pilot.
Merchant—one who buys " it " (*see* Commit Crashery).

Hot Air.—Is something which, if produced even to infinity, will never cut any ice—like this!

Oliver Doodar.—*See* " Flat Spin," which was this pilot's pet " stunt."

Stunt.—*See* " Split-ace Merchant "—when in the air.

The remainder are fortunately entirely expurgated.

R.A.F. EDUCATION SCHEME

A is for Azelot, our Aerodrome.
B stands for Boisdinghem, some time our home,
C for Cologne, the star show in May,
While D stands for Düren and bombing by Day.

E for Ehrange and "E.A." also,
F is for Frankfort, "a long way to go,"
While G for Gontrode, which is not far from Ghent,
And H is for "H.E." and Heule where it went.

I is for Iseghem, north of Courtrai,
And Jarville as J you'll find down Nancy way.
K Kaiserslautern, Koblenz, and Karlsruhe,
L for Liège and for Luxembourg too.

M Mons, Metz, Mannheim, to mention but three,
and N, of course, stands for our old friend Nancy.
O is for Ochey, from which one set out
To give "Pip" to Pirmasens and to the Pfalz Scout.

Q for Quercamps, which near Boisdinghem lay;
Rombas and "Roger" for R let us say.
S is for Strassburg, Saarbrück, and "Some Scrap";
T Thionville, Trèves (and now for the map!).

This one I can't find: it can be what U please.
V is Valenciennes and Vezelise.
A "Wash-out" is W (so are these rhymes).
X Xirocourt, where one dined many times.

Y is for Ypres, from the air what a view!
Z is Zweibrücken, which means "Bridges two."
If ever a parent you happen to be
Your children can learn the above A. B. C.
But beware of the N. Esses. Pip. Double C.
(N.S.P.C.C.)

NOTE.—The above is attributable to the one-time Education (?) Officer at H.Q., 8th Brigade. He is no longer there!

III

GERTIE'S GAZETTE

TANTONVILLE TIMES

Tune: "Really? Yes! Would you believe it?" from "Yes, Uncle."

There is in this Squadron a man with a brain.
 Really? Yes! Would you believe it?
The Latin word's "cranium," hence the word Crane.
 Really? Yes! Would you believe it?
Pelman and others are out of it quite,
For Sticky's a method that works out all right.
He develops his brain with some "Pyro" each night.
 Really? Yes! Would you believe it?

 Really now would you believe it?
 Still you must take it or leave it.
  In his hut in the wood he sits "plotting" all day
  And he's rapidly wearing his hair all away;
  For "fixing" it now he tries "Hypo" they say.
 Really? Yes! Would you believe it?

The Intelligence Officer now has his verse.
 Really? Yes! Would you believe it?
I hope he won't think of me any the worse—
 Really? Yes! Would you believe it?
When I say that at first I was apt to confuse
The comic contraption that Sticky's narks use,
With a cooker for making intelligence news.
 Really? Yes! Would you believe it?

 Really now, would you believe it?
 Still you must take it or leave it.
  Of the sources of hot air I know two or three,
  But two of them here I find don't quite agree;
  There are Ovens and ovens, I clearly can see.
 Really? Yes! Would you believe it?

In a legend I've heard of a mythical pair.
Really? Yes! Would you believe it?
They were giants they say, no doubt filled with "hot air."
Really? Yes! Would you believe it?
They were always together like master and dog
And in deeds of great daring they went the whole hog.
The giants were twins and called Gog and Magog.
Really? Yes! Would you believe it?

Really now, would you believe it?
Still you must take it or leave it.
We've a couple right here, though a trifle more mild,
And in each case the giant is only a child,
And one's Dudley Palmer, the other is Wild.
Really? Yes! Would you believe it?

A notice now hangs on the C.O.'s blackboard—
Really? Yes! Would you believe it?
That Palmer and Collett and Williams and Ward—
Really? Yes! Would you believe it?—
Have each been awarded the French Croix de Guerre,
Subject, of course, to permission to wear,
And we're shortly expecting a French General here.
Really? Yes! Would you believe it?

Really now, would you believe it?
Still you must take it or leave it.
When the French General reads out the names on the list,
There'll be a fine scene that by none should be missed.
And Le Capitaine Collett will have to be kissed.
Really? Yes! Would you believe it?

In the verse that I sang you on last Tuesday night—
  Really ? Yes ! Would you believe it ?
You find that my prophecy proved to be right.
  Really ? Yes ! Would you believe it ?
It certainly was a fine sight that we saw.
The Squadron paraded and the gallant four,
Apparently thinking " Gee whiz ! What a war ! "
  Really ? Yes ! Would you believe it ?

  Really now, would you believe it ?
  Still you must take it or leave it.
    We all of us saw, to our very great joy,
    Each one of them kissed—and they did look so coy—
    And we think the French General's a jolly old boy.
  Really ? Yes ! Would you believe it ?

You've all of you noticed our excellent guest.
  Really ? Yes ! Would you believe it ?
His name's Major Tedder ; he's one of the best.
  Really ? Yes ! Would you believe it ?
As 70's C.O. we knew him last May,
He had " Sop " two-seaters till they went away
To give place to the " Camel " which they fly to-day.
  Really ? Yes ! Would you believe it ?

  Really now, would you believe it ?
  Still you must take it or leave it.
    To the land of the Nile, to Egypt he's bound.
    I've been there myself, but I never once found
    Any camels at all that could get off the ground.
  Really ? Yes ! Would you believe it ?

We've done some good raids and we're proud of it too.
  Really ? Yes ! Would you believe it ?
We started the year by a raid on Karlsruhe.
  Really ? Yes ! Would you believe it ?

Three visits at least both to Trèves and Mannheim.
To Freiburg and Stuttgart we gave a bad time,
And Kaiserslautern, which I bet *you* can't rhyme.
  Really? Yes! Would you believe it?

  Really now, would you believe it?
  Still you must take it or leave it.
    The best of them all in p'raps every sense
    Were the times that we visited Mainz and Coblenz,
    And the Watch on the Rhine got some very bad
      dents!
  Really? Yes! Would you believe it?

On Roger was written a topical verse.
  Really? Yes! Would you believe it?
A libel, perhaps, but concise and terse.
  Really? Yes! Would you believe it?
Yet the purists insist that though rhythm and rhyme
Were possibly suited to both place and time,
The tale of a dog was by no means sublime.
  Really? Yes! Would you believe it?

  Really now, would you believe it?
  Still you must take it or leave it.
    They said it was doggerel and very crude.
    Dogmatic opinions I think are most rude.
    So I've doggedly dodged. I allude and elude.
  Really? Yes! Would you believe it?

MEMORANDA

Tune: "Three Hundred and Sixty-five Days all go to make a Year."

For the Wing we belong to, I've written this song to
Remind them that we
Are their brightest jewel, pride of Colonel Newell,
It's present O.C.
By night though One *Hundred,* is now the Hun's one dread
As we are by day,
And so in reprisal, we Squadrons comprise all
That there is to say.

100 and 55 both are out to bomb the Hun,
Both Squadrons belong to the Wing that is known as "41."
But kindly remember from May to September
That summer-time means longer days.
So the night-flier scores over the D.H.4's,
And the longer in bed each day stays.

100 and 55 both are out to bomb the Hun,
Both Squadrons belong to the Wing that is known as "41."
But kindly remember from May to September
In summer the weather is fine.
So they'll give a good time to all towns like Mannheim
And wind up the Watch on the Rhine.

100 and 55 both are out to bomb the Hun,
Both Squadrons belong to the Wing that is known
as "41."
But kindly remember from January to December
The chances of leave may be few,
So if none is at hand you just simply "forced-land,"
And stay there a week or p'raps two!

100 and 55 both are out to bomb the Hun,
Both Squadrons belong to the Wing that is known
as "41."
But kindly remember from now to November
If x be the number of shows,
Then the number of tons they will drop on the Huns
Any student of Algebra knows.

NOTE.—The answer to the last verse for all Squadrons of the Independent Force from October, 1917, to November, 1918, thirteen months, proved to be 508 raids, approximately 666 tons, or 1,491,588 lbs. of bombs.

IN FORMATION

Tune: " Widows are Wonderful," from " Yes, Uncle."

On your first formation
  In a D.H.4,
You'll have a sensation
  You've not had before.

You may think you're " Split-ace," [1]
  And all that sort of rot;
But try some close formation,
  And you'll learn a lot.

Our bus is wonderful, you must
  Admit that's true,
My lad, I'm telling you,
  And the Rolls-Royce in her, too.

Our bus is marvellous, of course,
  It has to be.
It's a D.H.4, I need say no more, but—Thumbs up,
  That's all!

Our bus is dangerous, the Huns
  Know us quite well, Mannheim,
Coblenz, Mainz, and all the rest.

To the Rhine when it's fine
  Come along with us 99
And bomb away every day.
  As we've done all this year.

[1] See Expurgated Glossary.

CONFIDENTIAL REPORT

Tune: "In other Words," (adapted) from "Bing Boys."

He's a fellow of undoubted great ability;
  As a pilot he is safe and he is sound.
In the air he flies, preserving his stability,
  And you never find him stunting near the ground.
His use of D.H.4's is economical.
  He rarely does a thing that would be rash.
And it strikes one as a matter almost comical,
  To suppose that for a moment he would crash.
He's a specialist at altitude photography,
  As a leader of formations he's I.T.,
Equipped with a good knowledge of topography,
  And we call him (with respect, of course) . . . "Fifi."

PERSONALITIES

Tune: " In other Words," from " Bing Boys."

Now all of you've met him wherever you've been
And heard him discourse on the war.
He culls his ideas from some column he's seen
In the *Times* of the Sunday before.
He's an expert (?) in all things on which one can speak
(His knowledge is probably nil),
While " straight from the nosebag " his facts (?) somehow leak.
He makes every moleheap a hill.

He is noted for grandiloquent verbosity,
With redundancy his parlance is replete.
He's a victim to colossal curiosity,
While all rumours and all scandals he'll repeat.
If you're wanting any news disseminating,
You will only have to whisper in his ear,
And leave it to his powers of demonstrating
That he's full of . . . " hot air."

As a brand-new observer I've come out to France
As green as the grass in the Spring,
Though ambition is great I have never a chance
Of doing a single brave thing.
To be Orderly Officer falls to my lot,
The 'phone to the C.O. is " dud ";
The language he uses makes me feel hot,
And he tells me my surname is mud.

He's a gentleman of fluctuating temperament.
  At times you'll find him charming and all's well;
At other moments, rather to your detriment,
  He'll curse you and consign your soul to h . . l.
When he tells you that you're something rather
    scarlet,
  Don't worry, for it's untrue, as you know;
A subaltern must ever be a varlet,
  So "Carry on" . . . in other words, C.O.

NOTE.—C.O.=Commanding Officer.
F.O.=Flying Officer.

121

A VEZELISE LULLABY

Tune: " Hush-a-bye, Baby."

Hush-a-bye, A.P., indents can wait,
Squadron's E.O.'s are a breed that you hate.
Why should you worry? Let the lot rip!
Hush-a-bye, A.P., sleepy Ack Pip.

SHOP

Tune: " Riding down to Bangor in an Eastern Train."

Sing a song of Aircraft used in the Great War,
Can you beat the record of the D.H.4?
  Eighteen months' hard service, and still going strong,
  She may see the War out, if it's not too long.

Sing a song of engines, we use a Rolls-Royce,
Thank your stars, ye Pilots, let your hearts rejoice.
  You have the " 8 Eagle," horse-power three-fifty,
  Lucky that it isn't a " Puma B.H.P."

Sing a song of Pilots from the Pilots' Pool,
Were it not for this War, they would be at school.
  For more information youth at all times yearns,
  Flying " in formation " here each Pilot learns.

Sing a song of crashes on the aerodrome,
Think of all the " hot air " that there is at home.
  But on active service it's another thing.
  Ack Eff double something send it to the Wing.

Sing a song of Squadrons, there's only one—our own.
When the War is over, and the truth is known,
  All the raids on Hunland surely will derive
  Fame for the old Squadron, No. 55.

THE OBSERVER'S ORISON TO HIS PILOT,

OR A BALLAD FROM THE BACK-SEAT

Tune: "Think of Me" chorus from "Yes, Uncle."

Think of me when your pressure's falling,
  And you're almost stalling off the ground:
Think of me when your engine's stuttering,
  And my heart is fluttering at the beastly sound.
Think of me when you crash on landing
  And your "understanding" comes away.
Say you always think of me,
  For I'm thinking of you all day.

OH, CECIL!

Tune: "The 5.15."

Look at all those fellows, clad in pale blue,
Aren't they awful dressy, don't you like the hue?
Surely they should not be wandering round the land,
Members of some uninterned Hungarian band.
They are not musicians, nor commissionaires—
You mustn't judge a person by the things he wears.
I asked one for a taxi, and he feigned that he was deaf,
So I guess he is a member of the R.A.F.

Chorus:

Fifty-five! Won't you sing this chorus.
Fifty-five! Come on, shout it loud.
Fifty-five! None is classed before us.
Best of all the Squadrons in the IF.RAF crowd.

The visit paid to Darmstadt made the Huns quite cross;
They nearly got a bull's-eye on the Ducal Schloss.
The Kaiser, too, was angry, remembering the time
They missed him by an hour when they bombed Mannheim,
But had he only waited he might have really won
The title of All Highest, and he might have hit the sun!
But the Horrid Hohenzollern knows one thing now quite well,
His direction is not skyward, but the shortest road to —Holland.

Chorus: Fifty-five! etc.

Think of all the bomb raids done by 55.
Isn't it a marvel that any Hun's alive?
Think of all the misses! Think also of the hits!
Think of the munition train they blew to little bits.
Give a thought to Frankfort, to Bonn give one or two,
And Trèves, Coblenz, and Düren, and don't forget
Karlsruhe.
Think of Ludwigshafen, where poison-gas was made,
In volume only rivalled by the " hot air " from Brigade.

Chorus: Fifty-five! etc.

What about a word now for old 99?
They did jolly good raids round about the Rhine.
Also we must mention Squadron one oh four,
They were too at Azelot and helped to win the war.
At Bettoncourt were stationed Squadron one one oh—
But all this is a memory, it is so long ago.
" Sic transit " for the Squadrons which now have passed
away,
" Air transit for the mails," the others do to-day.

Chorus: Fifty-five! etc.

POSTSCRIPT

It is hoped that, failing all other purposes, this volume will prove of use to all ex-members of The Squadron when asked by their children, " And what did you do in the Great War, Daddy ? "

15680086R00082

Printed in Great Britain
by Amazon